AIRBORNE
AT THE
END OF THE EARTH

Airborne at the End of the Earth is a terrific firsthand account of the professional airmanship challenges—as well as the emotional and spiritual ones—that come as a part of the daily job for hundreds of missionary pilots and their support teams, who fly in the most challenging environments on earth.

Make no mistake, this is not just a great read for pilots. It weaves together compelling aspects of family, culture, faith, and, yes, professional airmanship, in a manner that helps the reader understand the men and women who choose to take up this cross and how they do it both safely and professionally.

—Dr. Tony Kern
Founder & CEO, Convergent Performance
author of *Redefining Airmanship*

Having served in Asia for nine years, I grew to love the people there. I'm inspired by the commitment of Christians to proclaim God's Word and the openness of those hearing it to receive what it has to offer. Through this book, we all have the opportunity to meet the people in this beautiful, bountiful region.

As a missionary pilot to Papua for over twenty years, Nate Gordon gives readers both a bird's-eye view and an on-the-ground account of how the gospel is transforming lives there.

This powerful inside look at Bible translation in one of the most remote and linguistically diverse parts of our world is filled with hope. I pray it will inspire a new generation of Christians to go all-in to ensure God's Word is available to everyone, everywhere.

—Dr. John Chesnut
President & CEO, Wycliffe Bible Translators USA

I had the privilege of flying in Papua as a pilot with Mission Aviation Fellowship for a number of years. Nate Gordon's creative, insightful, and accurate depiction of life and ministry in this often forgotten part of the world quickly transported me back to a season of life that was full of purpose and challenge.

Papua is a land of contrasts. Beautiful pristine jungle gives way to foreboding mountains and rapidly changing weather patterns. Isolated tribes living in incredibly remote conditions are faced with profound physical and spiritual brokenness, yet there are those who are dedicating their lives to bring God's Word and the transformative truth found within it to a people who are deeply loved by Him.

This book will expand your understanding of this very special part of God's creation and the men and women who are utilizing unique tools and talents to reach those who have yet to understand the truth of the gospel. Through Nate Gordon's writing you will see a clearer picture of the heart of our Savior who is willing to seek out even one lost sheep.

—David Holsten
President & CEO, Mission Aviation Fellowship

These stories are potent and hope-filled. Nate's words draw stunning pictures of the wonder experienced by obedient servants who bring the Word of God to those living in remote and difficult places. The hunger for the good news etched across the faces of those who live in these distant corners of God's amazing creation is a modern-day Macedonian call to Christians: "Come over and help us."

These accounts of Nate and Sheri Gordon's experience serving our Savior in Papua are both heart-wrenching and heartwarming. They remind us that the best things in life are often the hardest, but serving our Savior open-handedly, holding on to nothing but Him, releases us to experience life to the fullest!

—Dr. Brent Slater
Senior Pastor, Highland Park Baptist Church
Southfield, Michigan

I love the "RFA" [Ready for Anything] attitude portrayed in many of Nate's stories, and I would recommend this book for anyone going to a mission field.

—Frans Sahureka
Director, YAJASI Aviation

If you've ever wondered what day-to-day life is like as a missionary pilot, read Nate Gordon's book. It made me appreciate the dangers, toils, and snares he lived through. It shows not only the practical side of life, but also the heart of a person who wants to take the message of the gospel to those who have yet to hear it. Reading this will make you want to live fully surrendered to whatever mission God has given you.

—Chris Fabry
Author and host of *Chris Fabry Live* on Moody Radio

AIRBORNE
AT THE
END OF THE EARTH

God's Word is reaching the most isolated people on the planet.
He's using airplanes to do it.

———

Nate Gordon

Airborne at the End of the Earth: God's Word Is Reaching the Most Isolated People on the Planet. He's Using Airplanes to Do It.
Copyright 2021 Nate Gordon

Bible version
All scripture quotations are from the Holy Bible, New International Version®, NIV®. Copyright © 1973, 1978, 1984, 2011 by Biblica, Inc.™ Used by permission of Zondervan. All rights reserved worldwide. www.zondervan.com The "NIV" and "New International Version" are trademarks registered in the United States Patent and Trademark Office by Biblica, Inc.™

Cover photo courtesy of Tim Harold

ISBN: 978-0-578-31618-5

CONTENTS

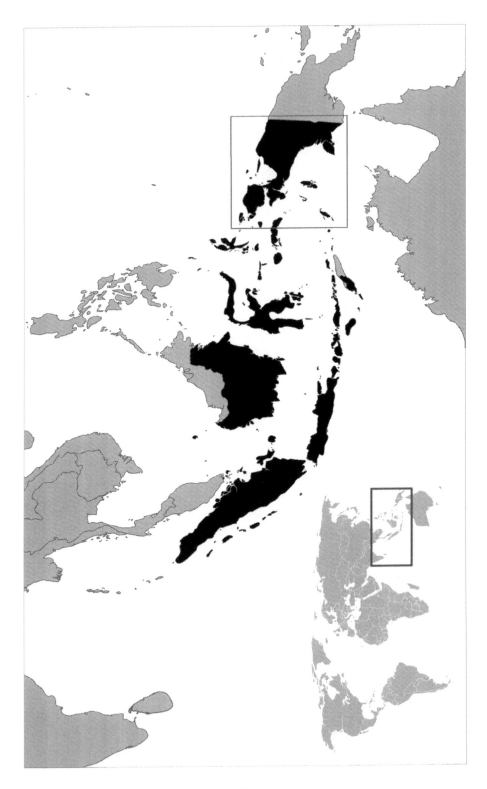

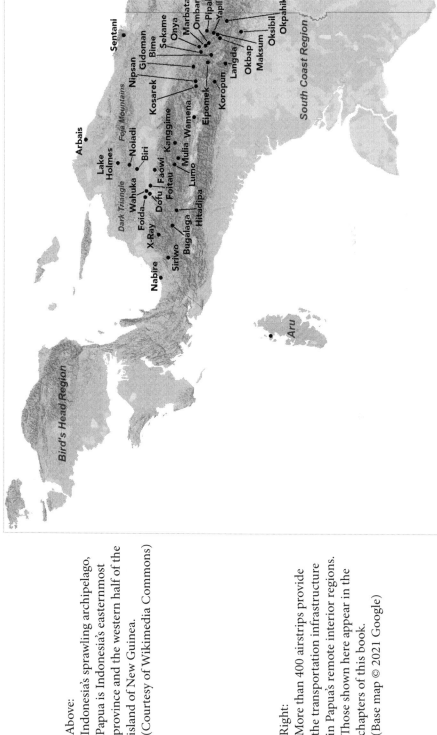

Above:
Indonesia's sprawling archipelago, Papua is Indonesia's easternmost province and the western half of the island of New Guinea.
(Courtesy of Wikimedia Commons)

Right:
More than 400 airstrips provide the transportation infrastructure in Papua's remote interior regions. Those shown here appear in the chapters of this book.
(Base map © 2021 Google)

FOREWORD

Ten years ago, I had the privilege of visiting Papua, Indonesia. A day spent flying into the remote airstrips in the interior of this vast island was the highlight of my trip. My pilot that day is now my dear friend and colleague Nate Gordon.

An hour's flight found us deep in Papua's Star Mountains, about to land on a grass runway literally carved out of the side of a mountain. We landed going uphill. After landing, under the wing of the aircraft, I met men who shared with me their way of life before the gospel reached this isolated valley. Nate translated for me since we didn't share any common language. These men spoke of living with constant fear of powerful spirits and ongoing, deadly violence between neighbors. One showed me an arrow wound on his neck from a battle in the days before they accepted Christ. Now these men are my brothers in Jesus. Their embrace of the gospel had transformed them into men of peace, and God's Spirit shone through them.

The gospel that transformed these men made its way to these remote valleys the same way I had: on aircraft flown by missionary pilots. In these pages Nate shares the story of what it means to bring God's Word to some of the most isolated people on the planet—using an airplane. I was privileged to witness this story in person for a day. This book gives me a much better appreciation for the depth of ministry that is happening day in and day out through the use of mission aviation in the service of reaching the ends of the earth.

This is a book to savor and to share. I couldn't put it down. Nate shares many amazing, faith-building stories of God's love working in the hearts and lives of people created in his image. If you wonder whether God is really at work in the world today, read this book. You will come away encouraged and amazed.

—Woody McLendon
President, JAARS Inc.
Waxhaw, North Carolina
November 2021

INTRODUCTION

The muffled hum of the jet engines was interrupted only by hints of quiet conversation and the pleasant sound of silver touching china. Five and a half miles above the Pacific Ocean, my wife, Sheri, and I found ourselves in the upper deck of a Boeing 747, enjoying cabin service in first class. Across the aisle sat our friend Dave Berdan, a pilot with the airline. By escorting us, he insured we were weren't paying a cent for the silver and china. It was the summer of 1996, and we were headed to Asia. Our initial destination was the Philippines. Twenty-seven years earlier, Sheri's parents had crossed this same ocean, also headed to the Philippines. They, on the other hand, sailed on a decrepit freighter that listed for the entire three-week journey.

I tried to feel guilty but couldn't quite pull it off.

Two weeks later, Sheri would be washing our clothes in a river, and I'd be getting familiar with the inside of a mosquito-infested outhouse—dysentery compelling my frequent presence there. We spent three months in the Philippines, training to live and work in some of the extremes that Asia had to offer.

After completing our time in the Philippines, we pushed off to Indonesia and settled in the city of Bandung, West Java. We lived there for nine months, learning to speak Indonesian.

When we'd finished our language training, we moved roughly 2,500 miles further east, to the far end of the Indonesian archipelago, to the place that had been our reason to board that first-class cabin almost a full year earlier: the town of Sentani in what was then known as Irian Jaya (now Papua).

A sleepy outpost town on the edge of the wilderness, Sentani's rough and tumble collection of tin roofs meandered aimlessly along the shores of the large lake from which the town derived its name. A single dusty main street ran from one end of town to the other, tracing the base of Mount Cyclops, which towered over Sentani like a watchful giant.

Sheri with friends in Bandung, West Java, ca. 1996. We spent nine months in Bandung learning the Indonesian language.

We'd come to the foot of Mount Cyclops to join a team of missionary pilots working with an organization called YAJASI. From a base at the Sentani airport, YAJASI's team operates light aircraft to reach out to the 270 different people groups scattered throughout Papua's vast interior. A strategic partner of Wycliffe Bible Translators and JAARS, YAJASI's vision is to see the lives of these Papuans transformed as they encounter their Creator through access to the Bible in their own language. In pursuit of this vision, the YAJASI team performs approximately 3,500 flights a year, making it possible for Bible translators and other mission workers to live and work among these isolated peoples.

Located just south of the equator and constituting the western half of the island of New Guinea, Papua is roughly the same size as California. The similarities end there. For starters, no roads connect the outside world to Papua's vast areas of lowland rainforest and towering mountain ranges. Instead, a half century of mission work has spurred the creation of a network of several hundred extremely simple runways that serve as portals to this isolated world.

YAJASI's base of operations at the foot of Mount Cyclops
(Photo courtesy of Glenn Grubb)

Through these portals—short, rough, often steeply sloped airstrips—came men and women seeking to penetrate the unknowns of Papua's interior. They came not seeking treasure or territory, but with hopes of bringing light where there was darkness, peace where there was killing, health where there was sickness, and understanding where there was superstition. Theirs are the real stories of Papua, stories of God using imperfect emissaries to make a profound difference in a place most of the world hardly knows exists.

More fascinating yet are the stories of individual Papuans who, living in a world just emerging from the Stone Age, allowed their hearts to be captured by the good news these outsiders brought. In countless cases, their lives, and the lives of their communities, have been transformed.

In the two decades we served in Papua, it was Sheri's and my honor to get to know people from both of these groups—those bringing lit torches, and those in darkness who took those torches and carried them onward.

I can recount only the all-too-brief moments where our lives intersected on my airplane or on some remote jungle airstrip. However brief and fragmented those encounters, my hope in telling these stories is that they will provide pull-back-the-curtain glimpses of the beauty, wonder, and rich character of our God; remind us of the unparalleled sense of meaning that's available to us when we obey this God—even when that obedience is tainted, timid, and tepid; and inspire some of us to follow the example of simple, anonymous saints, unknown to the world, heroes of heaven.

Nate, Sheri, and Cameron Gordon (1999)

—Nate Gordon
Waxhaw, North Carolina
November 2021

1

HIPPO

To belong to Jesus is to embrace the nations with him.
—JOHN PIPER

The only constant in the life of a jungle pilot in Papua is that no day looks anything like another. Some days I drag myself home wondering how I got myself into this racket. Most days I can't believe that I actually get to do this stuff. I have yet to become immune to the wonder of climbing into a machine that transports me to a world completely off the map … the aeronautical equivalent of C.S. Lewis's wardrobe door.

Today, I started out from our home base in Sentani in a Helio Courier* full of cargo: supplies for the Dority family working at a post called Biri, and building materials for the Brileys who are translating the Bible for the Bauzi people in a place called Noiadi. I stopped at the tiny village of Biri first. Clusters of open-sided huts line the airstrip here, their roofs a beautiful pattern of woven palm fronds. Opening the door of the airplane, I stepped into the stifling air of the hot and humid lowlands—a reminder of why the Biri-Tai people build wall-less homes. I had a pleasant chat with Carolyn Dority and her kids as I was unloading their stuff. Her husband, Dan, was out trekking through the jungle, visiting isolated hamlets with local evangelists. The kids said that the dog had eaten one of the two kittens I had brought them on my last trip.

The other kitten was still kicking. I could see why the dog wouldn't touch it—the little guy was covered with ringworm and mange. The jungle is tough on kitties. After the unloading was done, Carolyn asked if I would pray for rain. Like most missionaries' jungle homes, the only water supply comes from rain off their roof.

I'm soon strapping in for the short flight to Noiadi. Takeoff at Biri is always a bit of a trick. You're parked on a little flat area at the top of a steeply sloped hill that's only about 200 feet long (envision an excellent sledding hill). At the bottom of the hill, the airstrip decides to go flat again—the way any well-behaved airstrip ought to be in the first place. The problem is that you build up a frightful momentum barreling down the sloped section, and if the airplane isn't ready to fly by the time you get to the bottom, you splat into the flat section in a manner that, while not hurting the airplane, damages the carefully cultivated image of pilots being in complete control of their flying machines.

The Helio Courier climbs the steep section on the Biri airstrip.
(Photo courtesy of Tim Harold)

Today, with the Doritys' stuff offloaded, the airplane is light and, by holding my tongue just right, we manage to get airborne quickly enough to avoid the nonsense at the bottom of the hill.

Noiadi is just 10 minutes away. After overflying the airstrip to make sure the Bauzis know I'm coming, I power back and lower the airplane down into the canyon. I fly the approach hugging the side of a cliff face until turning final. Final approach lowers you farther down into the canyon, and soon you're committed to land: You reach a point where you simply can't abandon the approach because you can't outclimb or outturn the terrain—an airborne point of no return. Practically speaking, this means that if a pig, dog, or cassowary runs out onto the airstrip, they are, in the vernacular, *toast*. If a person runs out onto the airstrip, well then, you're now faced with a relatively complex ethical decision … and about a half second in which to make it.

Noiadi. There are very few places in Bauzi territory suitable for an airstrip. This island in a river bend provided a place to put Noiadi's 365-meter-long runway.

Today, dogs, pigs, and people behave themselves and stay off the airstrip. Dave and Joyce aren't in the village at this time, but the Bauzi people are busy continuing the community development project that the Brileys have started. The Bauzis are a fun-loving lot and, though we can't communicate much (my Bauzi is lousy and their Indonesian[1] is almost as bad), we have a ball unloading the tin roofing and nails. I play the bumbling novice and they, having seen these airplanes for years—but probably never a bicycle—are keen to show me how to operate the Helio's cargo door. I ask directions to my next stop, and five guys simultaneously give me loud, urgent, and profoundly contradictory directions to Lake Holmes. I love these guys. I give a hesitant assurance that I can find my way there, and they turn to the task of loading the airplane up with sacks of peanuts—another product of a community development project. Back in Sentani, the peanuts will be sold at the market, and the proceeds sent back to the people of Noiadi.

After positioning the Helio at the very end of the airstrip, I look for signs of a breeze in the tops of the sago palms that line the jungle runway. With the canyon wall a few hundred yards off the end of the strip, you don't need a tailwind* to make the takeoff any more interesting. Standard procedure to avoid hitting the aforementioned rockface is to hang a left shortly after liftoff and follow the river downstream until you gain sufficient altitude to clear the ridges.

Lake Holmes will be my last stop of the day. The plan is to get some fuel. And a pig. By now it's close to midday, and cumulous clouds are building all around me. I fly the approach to Lake Holmes in light rain. Once on the ground, I inquire as to the whereabouts of the pig. It's coming, I'm told. In the meantime, I accommodate two requests to take pictures of people for their government marriage certificate applications. With kids and babies hanging all over them, they look effectively married to me. They also bring me an older lady who is bleeding at the gums and hasn't eaten in a week. I take notes and promise to consult with the doc and dentist back in town. (That evening the diagnosis was

---

1 The national language of Indonesia is called Bahasa Indonesia—generally referred to as Indonesian in English. In Papua, Bahasa Indonesia serves as a trade language for indigenous Papuans, who speak 270 different languages.

scurvy, so I brought her salt for rinses and some vitamin C on my next trip.) The people bring me small wads of money, motheaten and tattered, and their shopping lists: razors, batteries, a ballpoint pen...

When all have been tended to, I sit down in the dirt under the airplane wing with a ragtag bunch of people I'm proud to call my friends. Two different people groups live at Lake Holmes: highland Danis who came with the first missionaries, who hiked into the area back in the late 1960s, and the Bauzi tribe, whose territory sprawls for hundreds of square miles around the lake. Countless times the shade of the airplane wing has provided a comfortable place to hang with my Papuan brothers and sisters. Jokes are swapped, prayers prayed, stories told, and disputes settled as the aluminum over our heads keeps the intense tropical sun at bay.

I will never forget the time when, sitting in this very same dirt under the very same wing, a Bauzi woman in a dress so filthy that I'm sure it's her one and only, comes over and, with fingers as dirty as her dress, hands me a charred fish on a banana leaf, right off the fire. I was stunned and honored. And hungry. Honestly, it was one of the most delicious meals I'd had in a while. While I ate, the folks sitting around me held a quiet conversation in Bauzi. When there were only bones left on the banana leaf, I asked what they'd been talking about. Petrus, a soft-spirited Bauzi elder who speaks fairly decent Indonesian, tells me how meaningful it is to them that I have eaten their food.

I thought, *What? You bring me a delicious fish that you could have eaten yourself, and, somehow, by enjoying your selflessness, this makes* me *the good person?*

Petrus shares a little deeper with me, and the picture becomes clearer. His people often feel ridiculed because of their "backwardness." To have a foreigner from the "developed" world sit in the dirt, eat their food, with his hands, just like they do, transmits a message of worth and dignity that no amount of preaching can convey.

I need to eat more fish.

Back in the present, there's a lull in the conversation. I pull myself to my feet and wander out to the airstrip to get a better look at the weather for my route home. Light rain is still falling, and the weather doesn't look encouraging … grumpy at best. I glance towards the village. Several Danis are pushing, pulling, poking, and generally cajoling an unhappy hippopotamus down the hill towards the airstrip. Looks like hard work. Then it hits me. This is the first hippo I've seen in Papua … matter of fact, I don't recall reading anything about the existence of hippos in Papua … or in Asia for that matter. In my head, I begin drafting a piece for the biology journals.

Alas, there will be no lecture tours for me. To my chagrin, as the noisy beast gets closer, I can see that the hippo is actually the mythical *porcus monstrum*—a monster pig. Papua veterans later told me they had never seen a pig so large. To quote the chagrined fellow who received the beast at the end of the flight: "Nate, I asked you to bring me a pig, not a cow!"

There had been some talk about taking this pig out alive. I told the people in no uncertain terms that the pig and I were not both getting into the same airplane alive. In the ensuing discussion, it was decided that the pig would be the one to make the trip sans head. My friend

Working with Weinus, our faithful agent in Lake Holmes—the man
who shot the monster pig

Weinus uses only one arrow to fell the massive animal. Right through the heart. They finish the task in record time. In the jungle, tarps are made out of banana leaves, and one is quickly put together to protect the floor of the Helio. It takes six grown men to muscle the monster into the airplane—he's over 6 feet long, without his head.

It's about 1:30 in the afternoon, I'm finally climbing out over the lake and pointing the Helio's nose towards home. It's just me, some peanuts, and the hippo. I'm soon clear of the rain and have an hour and a half flight over the immense spread of jungle and mountain. It gives me time to think about how God is slowly, persistently, reaching the isolated people of Papua with his love.

There's also time to pray that rain will fill the barrels in Biri.

2

X-RAY

Oh, to grace how great a debtor daily I'm constrained to be.
—Robert Robinson

Checkpoint X-Ray. Even the name has the ring of adventure. Three fast-flowing cataracts tumble out of these remote mountains, joining together to form a single river that rushes north to the plains before slowly meandering to the coast. The confluence of the three rivers forms an unmistakable X. Early missionary pilots christened the easily recognizable landmark Point X-Ray. The name stuck and to this day pilots use X-Ray as a reporting point.

The terrain in X-Ray's four valley systems is simple—it goes one of two directions: up or down, and not in a very disciplined manner. From the peaks, the mountain walls descend steeply to the river's edge. Clinging to these slopes are small clusters of huts and garden clearings, the people of X-Ray. They're called the Moi.[2] Choosing to stay within the relative safety of X-Ray's valleys, the Moi entered the twenty-first century as one of the very few completely uncontacted people groups left on the planet.

---

2 When I first wrote of our experiences in X-Ray, I used the term *Maniwo* for the people. As evidence of how little we knew about these people, this term turned out to be incorrect—it is a word used by outsiders for the people of X-Ray's valleys. The people refer to themselves as the Moi (pronounced moy).

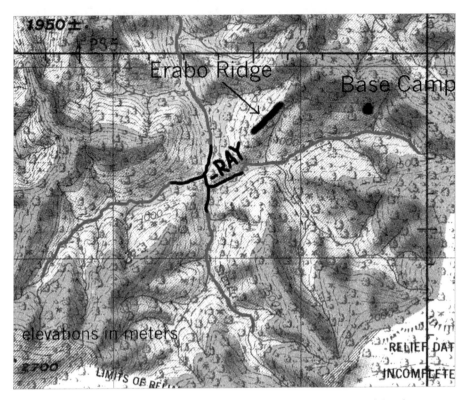

The X-Ray valley chart. Note "Relief Data Incomplete" in the lower righthand corner. When I first began flying in Papua, the available charts contained numerous blank spots, indicating terrain that had yet to be charted.

Working among the neighboring Auye (ow-yay) people, Mike Moxness had long heard stories of people living in the valleys east of him. His hands more than full with his outreach to the Auye, Mike prayed for the day when others might be able to reach the Moi with the gospel of Jesus. In 1999, Mike led the first helicopter forays into X-Ray's western valley to try to determine just who these people were. Part of the impetus for those first trips was that God had brought to Papua three young families from a like-minded organization who had caught a vision to reach the Moi. From Canada, Indonesia, and the United States, this diverse group was united by a serious case of X-Ray fever. Mike saw in this team the answer to his prayers.

From those first brief helicopter trips, it became quickly apparent that a major obstacle to reaching the Moi would be finding a suitable site on which to build an airstrip. Without an airstrip, these families wouldn't be able to live in the X-Ray valley, and the Moi would not have the opportunity to hear of the treasure of Jesus. The families wanting to reach the Moi needed a portal.

And so, in July 2000, I found myself flying low and slow over X-Ray's valleys in one of our Helio Couriers. Another of our pilots, Syd Johnsen, sat next to me, clipboard and portable GPS in hand. In the back, keenly scanning the terrain below, were Anderson Panambunan, Tim Whatley, and Steve Crockett, the men of the three families hoping to bring the good news to the Moi. We carefully surveyed all four valley systems in X-Ray, using the GPS to plot sites that appeared to have airstrip potential. Though we identified about eight points that bore further looking into, there were only two that showed any real promise. One was a ridge close to the actual X. The other was near a fairly large settlement with expansive gardens in the eastern valley.

We spent the night in the coastal town of Nabire (na bee ray) where Tim's dad, Bonard, joined us. The next day Syd shuttled the team and supplies in the Helio to the Auye village of Siriwo—the closest airstrip to the Moi territory. We spent the following night in the Moxnesses's simple home in Siriwo. The camaraderie on the team was superb; the quality of cannibal jokes, not so good. Despite the high spirits of the evening, I'm not sure any of us slept much that I night—I know I didn't. There was too much anticipation of what tomorrow might hold.

First light found us back on the airstrip waiting for Helimission's* helicopter to arrive. Soon the Bell Long Ranger was on the ground, and Brian Smith piled out smiling—that's pretty much a permanent condition for Brian, but I could tell he was pumped for today. A helicopter pilot with a passion for reaching the unreached, he lives for this kind of stuff. After hot refueling* the heli, I jumped in next to Brian. In the back, Tim and Steve were joined by Pinatus, an Auye man who we hoped could understand enough of the Moi language to act as an interpreter. For this first trip in, we kept the team small and took almost nothing with us so that the helicopter would be as light as possible.

We had decided to make our initial contact in the eastern valley where we had seen the larger cluster of huts. As we came over the little hamlet, we watched a dozen men, every one of them clutching their bows and arrows, scrambling for cover. The women, if there were any around, didn't show themselves.

Any hopes that we would easily find an airstrip site in these mountains died quickly as we watched Brian struggle to find a place to land. A hovering chopper can lower itself onto any reasonably flat surface, but in X-Ray's steep terrain and towering forest, finding a spot to set even a helicopter down was proving to be almost impossible. After two abortive approaches to gardens that refused to cooperate as helipads, we finally spotted a garden site that looked like it would work. Brian skillfully lowered us towards the tiny clearing. All manner of obstacles—trees, stumps, rocks, logs—were literally within feet of the chopper's main and tail rotors. I think we may have shortened a few banana trees with the main rotor.

A brief aside here: When a helicopter pilot says things like "Don't worry, it's soft wood," my own sentiment is that worrying should commence immediately. Another sure signal that it's time to crank up one's anxiety motor is when the pilot utters "uh-oh" under his breath.

I heard Brian release this two-syllable beauty as the helicopter descended the final few feet towards the ground for what I thought was going to be a landing—only to have the aircraft jerk to a stop, still suspended 2 feet above the garden floor. (To our man's credit, many a less pious helicopter pilot would have issued a string of one-syllabled beauties at this point.) I looked out my side and saw what had caused the "uh-oh." When one clears the jungle for a garden using a stone axe, one chops down trees at hip level—trees are hard enough to take out with a stone axe at that easy height, and no self-respecting stone-axe-person would bend himself in half to chop down a tree at its roots. Our left skid was wedged into the "y" of a tree trunk chopped down in such a manner. We hadn't seen the trunk prior to this because it was obscured by the huge elephant-ear leaves of the taro plants growing in the garden … that, and the fact that all of our senses were gainfully occupied worrying about hitting something harder than "soft wood."

Brian gently tugged upward on the flight controls. No go. We were caught in a curious trap. Tethered to the ground, we couldn't go up. Stuck in midair, we couldn't go down. We were suspended in an unnatural hover, two feet off the ground with obstacles very close to the main and tail rotors. I offered to get out and try to free us. Brian didn't say anything, just shook his head. (Later he told me that I would have likely upset the precarious balance of the helicopter … with unpleasant consequences.) Again, he tried. Again, no joy. Still stuck like a bird in a snare. On the third try there was a slight jolt and the helicopter slipped free of the tree stump. Brian moved us laterally about 18 inches and set the chopper down gently in the taro plants. The four of us, having resumed breathing, quickly clambered out into the garden.

Brian Smith lands the heli in the garden
(note the Moi man in the foreground).

The helicopter is an amazing machine. One minute we've got a visitor-at-a-museum perspective, safely looking down on a stone-age panorama—we might as well have been watching the Discovery Channel. Then, in the blink of an eye, we find ourselves standing in the exhibit. We've climbed through the TV screen. I remember it being quiet those first moments in the garden, which I know can't be right because the helicopter was still circling overhead—our lifeline in case things went bad in a *Through Gates of Splendor*[3] kind of way. I think my mind views those first minutes as silent because none of us spoke ... and there were no Moi to be seen anywhere. They had disappeared.

We didn't have to wait long. The green at the edge of the garden rustled, and a Moi man stepped into the clearing. He was unarmed, naked except for his gourd.[4] We were relieved that he was friendly and that the Moi greeting was an easy one: *Aba-aba.* Pinatus, the interpreter, tried to explain that we came in peace. He was visibly shaking as he spoke. Up to this point, my only worries had been the ones I'd left behind in the helicopter. Seeing our Auye guide trembling, I briefly wondered if we ought to consider fear as the appropriate state of mind for the circumstances. Fortunately, there wasn't time to dwell on it. Seven or eight more Moi men, who had stayed in the shadows watching their brave friend, now slipped out of the jungle to greet us. Again, they were all unarmed. I wondered what they had done with their weapons. The handshakes were warm, the greetings heartfelt, and full of smiles. We knew but one simple word of the Moi language, aba-aba, and yet I was struck again by the universal message of warmth that a smile conveys. It fascinated me to think of what might have been running through the minds of these brave Moi as they left the safety of the jungle to meet the first outsiders they'd ever seen.

I had a handheld radio for communicating with Brian, who was still circling overhead. I told him that our first contact with the Moi had gone well and that he could head back to Siriwo to get Anderson and Bonard and start shuttling in supplies. He tells me that the last landing was about as much adventure as he can stand, and he won't return until we've cleared the obstacles from the garden. We needed Anderson, Bonard, and those supplies, so we needed to find a way to turn this obstacle-strewn garden into a safe helipad.

We've just made first contact with the warriors of an isolated tribe, and within minutes we need to tell them that we want to destroy part of

---

3 *Through Gates of Splendor* is the book by Elisabeth Elliot about five Christian missionary men martyred when making first contact with Waironi tribesmen in the Ecuadorian jungles in 1956.

4 Traditionally, in many Papuan people groups, men wore penis-gourds, which provided a modicum of modestly while at the same time serving to visibly proclaim their status as men.

Our first contact with the Moi people. Nate, Tim Whatley
(background, facing camera), and Pinatus (at right, with cap)

one of their gardens so that the helicopter can land without scaring the "uh-oh" out of the pilot again. Though we were wholly inexperienced in international diplomatic protocol, we knew that at best, we were royally blowing our entrance. At worst, we were about to give these guys a reason to go find their bows and arrows.

International trade came to the rescue. With foresight brought on no doubt by reading too many missionary biographies, Steve and Tim had brought along a stack of machetes. The Stone Age is pretty cool unless you happen to be the one using the stones. Try cutting through hardwood with sharpened pieces of rock. For the Moi, a machete's steel blade was perhaps the most valuable thing we could have offered them. Through sign language, we somehow communicated what we wanted and what we would give for it. It was clear to us that the Moi felt these crazy white guys had ridiculously underpriced the machetes—a few taro plants were nothing to pay for the magic tools. In no time, we and the Moi were working together in the spirit of international cooperation, feverishly clearing the site of stumps, logs, and even lopping off the top of a tree as the Moi took to the machetes like fish to water. It was at this point that the mystery of the absence of weapons was solved. As we cleared the site, rolling rocks and stumps into the jungle, we discovered that the Moi had left their bows and arrows hidden at the edge of the forest. They had taken pains to make sure we didn't feel threatened ... but were prudent enough to keep their weapons within easy reach.

The Moi we met were indeed friendly and very intent on making sure that we felt welcomed into their world. But there was a darkness to their countenances. It struck me as a mixture of fear and anger. The others noticed it too. Years later, it would be just as striking to me to see this darkness disappear. Gone. Replaced with a clear peace and an absence of fear. But I'm getting ahead of myself... We were, at the moment, completely concentrated on creating a safe, non-uh-oh-inducing place for Brian to land.

Soon, the helicopter was back. Our work on the helipad was apparently satisfactory enough to preclude any further stress to Brian's overworked adrenal glands. As part of the team set up camp, I set off with a couple of the others to survey the potential airstrip sites we had identified from the air.

Nate guiding Brian in for the second landing in the
X-Ray garden site

16

When walking through the jungle looking for a place where you might someday land an airplane, the two basic things one evaluates are length and slope. Lengthwise, we needed an absolute minimum of 300 yards. For slope, we can work with some pretty steep grades as long as the slope remains relatively consistent—meaning, roller coasters are out. Using a measuring tape and inclinometer*, we set about evaluating a particularly promising area we'd seen from the air. After a couple of hours of hacking through the jungle, it became apparent that, as good as it looked from the air, the terrain in this location held utter disregard for our tidy airstrip criteria.

A bit discouraged, we returned to camp in the late afternoon. Our spirits were soon lifted when we saw how much work Bonard had accomplished in setting up camp. Anderson, too, brought a smile to our faces. His indefatigable good nature was in full bloom. Hailing from the Indonesian province of Manado, Anderson was as far out of his element as the rest of us, but his passion for bridging the gap with these isolated people was unrivaled. His shirtless body had been covered in Moi war paint, and three or four Moi men were animatedly giving him instruction in their style of wrestling. I don't think Anderson won many matches, but he kept a notebook close at hand, which he was quickly filling up with Moi words. By now there were eleven or twelve Moi men sitting in and around our camp. They were absolutely fascinated with our stuff. Setting up my tent proved to be a big attention-getter. They brought us baked taro root, hot off the fire. We gave them oranges and noted how they carefully saved the seeds. Tim treated any open wounds they had. We were sincerely grateful for how warmly we had been received. Still, it gave us pause when occasionally groups of three or four would move off to a nearby hut and hold animated discussions. One man in particular, a late arrival to the proceedings, had been surly from the start and was obviously not happy with our presence.

Caked with sweat and mud from thrashing around on the mountain-side all day, we bathed in one of the bracingly cold streams near the camp. Someone cooked up some rice and we topped it with a mixture of dried fish and tofu we'd brought with us—sounds like it would taste awful. It does. But that evening, sitting under that tarp on that X-Ray hillside, I must say it was delicious. Since this was before the advent of affordable satellite phones, we had strung up an antenna for a portable HF[5] radio and were able to make contact with Steve's wife, Carolyn, back in Sentani and let her know all was well. We had a solid group of people there standing behind us in prayer.

Steve Crockett speaks with his wife, Carolyn, over
the HF radio on our first evening in the X-Ray valley.
(left: Tim Whatley; right of Steve: Bonard Whatley)

After dinner we all retired early. I shared a tent with Anderson. The ground was hard, and I was cold. Worse, all night little gnats called *agas* roamed freely around my sleeping bag delivering their needle-prick bites on my shivering flesh. I tossed and turned while Anderson lay peacefully still beside me. I felt like such a soft city boy who couldn't handle a night in the jungle, jealous of Anderson's Indonesian-bred toughness. The next morning, as we peeled ourselves out of the sleeping bags, I groggily asked Anderson if he'd slept well.

"Not a wink. Those stupid agas chewed on me all night long."

---

5 High frequency (HF) radio, sometimes called single-side band (SSB), uses a long cable strung between two poles as an antenna, for communicating over long distances where line of sight between stations isn't possible.

Anderson sure knew how to cheer up a self-doubting Westerner first thing in the morning. Still, the sleepless night made the morning's reality that much starker: we'd surveyed some of the most promising terrain in X-Ray and come up empty. Over breakfast and coffee, we planned our next steps. We decided that when Brian showed up with the helicopter, we'd head west to a ridge site that we had identified on the original aerial survey two days prior.

We soon heard the now-familiar whap-whap-whap of the Bell Long Ranger entering the valley. Four of us climbed in, and I explained to Brian where we needed to go. The ridge was just four miles west, and we were overhead in a few minutes. With the helicopter, we were able to do a much closer inspection of the ridge than is safely possible in a fixed-wing aircraft. As we flew up and down the ridgeline, we began to get excited about the potential of this site. It was the only piece of land we had seen that appeared to have a consistent slope over a reasonable length. The problem was that God had placed this prime spot in thick virgin forest on the top of a ridge—how to get in?

On an extremely narrow lower extension of the spine of the ridge, well below the main section we needed to survey, we spotted a small bald section of ridgeline. Brian thought it was worth a try. (He's either very good, or a bit nuts. A safe wager is that he's both.) After a couple of passes, he finally finds a spot he wants to try, but the ridge, if you can call it that, is so sharp that there is only enough room to get the front of his skids down on terra firma. I'm up front next to Brian, and he gives me explicit instructions that when the heli touches down, I am to roll out of the cockpit and lie down flat next to the skid. The only place I could have gone was uphill on the ridgeline—right into the spinning main rotor. Brian picked the heli up off the mountain, and once he was clear, I scrambled out of the way. He brought the bird back down again—this time balancing the rear of the skids on the ridge. Steve, Pinatus, and Tim piled out and went prone on the ridge until the helicopter lifted off again. As we gathered ourselves together to start hiking up the spine towards the main ridge, Brian hung around like an oversized insect buzzing overhead.

"Look up."

It's Brian's voice on my handheld radio. We raise our heads, and there he is flying by us with a video camera in one hand. If we slide off the edge, he doesn't want to miss his chance to film it.

His video fun done, Brian heads back to our camp where he'll spend the rest of the day waiting for us to call on the radio for a pickup. As we begin to hike upwards along the ridge, we see why the land here is bare: parts still show the blackened scars of a fire (probably from a lightning strike) that had swept it clean within the last couple of months. God had prepared a way for us in the wilderness. We paused for a moment and gave him thanks.

A hard climb brought us to the lower end of the main ridge, and we started taking our measurements. The average visibility through the jungle, after we had hacked out a trail, was about 14 yards. About an hour or so into the hike, we came across a break in the canopy which afforded me an opportunity to get a good GPS fix of our position. The others moved on ahead, cutting the path along the ridgeline. Alone, I stood in the small clearing waiting for the GPS to receive a signal. For some reason, the hair on the back of my neck stood up, and I sensed that I was no longer alone. I turned around and there, standing a few feet behind me, totally silent, was the ghostlike figure of a Moi man. Who knows how long he had followed us noiselessly through the forest? He must have seen the helicopter and clambered up the mountain from the small group of huts we'd seen in the valley on the west side of the ridge. We aba-aba'd each other and, not really knowing what to do, I reached into my fanny pack and gave him some licorice that my mom had sent me from the States. He loved it. *Licorice!* I had found a brother. Later, I learned his name was Piato. We found a way to communicate what we were doing, handed him a machete, and from there on out he led the way. He also told us that the ridge we were on was called Erabo.

Hours later it was apparent that Erabo Ridge was long enough, and the slope was workable. It was going to take more effort than I wanted to think about to turn this heavily forested ridgeline into a smooth, landable airstrip, but based on everything else we'd seen in X-Ray, this site held by far the most promise. Five grueling hours after being dropped off, we were back on the knife-edge ridge for the pickup. We climbed

Piato

back aboard the helicopter, praising God that he had given the Moi team an airstrip site.

My job done, I left the X-Ray valley and returned home, thinking that the story of finding an airstrip in X-Ray pretty much ended there.

It didn't.

A recurring theme in my life has been that whenever the question of credit and pride comes into play, God reminds me that my best efforts always fall short. The crazy thing is, he also has a way of taking my stumbling, often impurely motivated endeavors and using them anyway—and he does it in a way that always makes it clear to me that:

Apart from me you can do nothing.

If God's not part of it, most of what I touch turns into a pile of rocks. The corollary is that when I join God in what he's doing, he has a way of taking even my most flawed efforts and turning them into something good. The story of finding an airstrip in X-Ray was no exception.

The next day, as I hitched a ride from Nabire back to Sentani on a commercial operator's flight, Brian flew back to X-Ray and moved the team from our original campsite to a spot just below Erabo Ridge where a small number of Moi lived in a community called Daboto. Over the next months, as the team settled into the new area and began to build their houses, they periodically made hikes back up to Erabo to start planning the airstrip. On one of those hikes, it dawned on them that a piece of land they traversed on their way to Erabo might just work as an airstrip. A little more research confirmed the new site would indeed prove suitable. Not only was this site much closer to where the Moi team were building their homes, but it would entail far less work to turn it into an airstrip.

So, the airstrip didn't end up on Erabo Ridge after all. No matter how badly my self-interested spirit would want to take credit for helping the team find a place to put their airstrip, I couldn't. They found the place themselves.

And yet … a theme that runs through the story of God's interaction with his creation is his passion for redeeming things. As we look back on those first days in the X-Ray valley, we can see how God guided our imperfect efforts and placed the team in an absolutely strategic spot in Moi territory. In our complete ignorance of the Moi area at the time, we had no way of knowing just how perfect a location Daboto would turn out to be. While there are only a few Moi living in the Daboto hamlet, it turns out it's a sort of jungle crossroads for the entire X-Ray valley trail system. The Moi are a mobile people, and their journeys frequently take them through the central intersection at Daboto … which in turn enables the team to maintain contact with the many far-flung Moi communities throughout the X-Ray valley.

God used Erabo to draw us to Daboto.

Today, when I fly for the Moi team, I land on the Daboto airstrip in the shadow of Erabo Ridge. I look at that ridgeline, and I'm reminded of God's way with me.

3

THE DARK TRIANGLE

Turn to me and be saved, all you ends of the earth;
for I am God, and there is no other.
—Isaiah the Prophet

"House!" Duane screamed into the intercom. Ears ringing, I banked the aircraft in the direction Duane was pointing ... and surreptitiously turned down the volume on my headset. I soon spotted what had prompted Duane's assault on my eardrums. A single, tiny hut in a clearing in the dense blanket of the jungle below us.

"Score: Duane 22, Nate 3, Mark 0." The voice of lament on the intercom belonged to our back seat passenger, Mark. Duane was going to win this contest handily, clearly the best airborne hut hunter of the three of us. Tasked with keeping the airplane from an unhappy convergence with the trees, I cut myself a fair bit of slack, but Mark, on the other hand, was clearly not happy with the current state of affairs.

For millennia, mankind stood on the ground looking up at the sky, trying to scheme a way to get up there. As soon as man figured it out, we promptly began staring back down at the ground, looking for stuff. Aerial surveys have been used across a broad swath of disciplines: cartography, agriculture, conservation, geology. I remember doing a survey with a couple of geologists who, pointing at a cluster of perfect spheres of bubbling gray muck below me in the Papuan rainforest, told me that we were looking at the largest mud volcanoes in the southern hemisphere.

But, as far as aerial surveys go, this was a new one for me. The day before, Mark Donahue and Duane Clouse, both linguists, climbed into the Helio, and we set out on a three-day aerial survey looking for, of all things, hidden *people*.

I wondered if anywhere in the world that day there was another airplane aloft in search of previously undiscovered groups of human beings. Located in an area of Papua that some have called the Dark Triangle, our survey area covered approximately 2,000 square miles of territory, much of it essentially unexplored. Parts of the chart I had laying in my lap were literally blank—empty white spaces marked "Relief Data Incomplete." It was like flying into a huge question mark.

Much of the jungle we flew over was ruggedly inhospitable. "This terrain is *tortured*," is how Mark described the total absence of anything flat. Are there people living in this wilderness known only to God? If there are, who are they? What languages do they speak? Answering these questions was the goal of these flights. The ultimate objective was to reach any people living in these areas with the good news of Jesus and to give them the Word of God translated into their own language.

For the most part we followed rivers, scanning the banks for any signs of life: a hut, a canoe, a grove of sago palms…[6] At one point we flew low over a sandbar to check out what appeared to be human footprints. Mostly, we just stared at the endless green canopy of rainforest below.

The first day out, we were blessed with unusually clear weather over the Foja Mountains. This gave us a chance to survey a place high up in the Fojas that one of our pilots had christened Dinosaur Valley. In his words, "If there are dinosaurs left on the earth, they'll be living up there." A wide depression in the mountains guarded by a perimeter of rugged peaks, this isolated valley was almost always shrouded in clouds. Early in the morning, before the mountains had cloaked themselves in cloud, the Fojas revealed their secret place to us. There was a sense of invading a private sanctuary … stealing a glimpse into a forbidden garden that was meant to stay hidden.

---

6 For most lowland people groups in Papua, sago trees are the primary source of food. After felling the tree, a painstaking all-day process extracts a starchy powder from the palm's core. Chunks of the sago are either roasted on the fire or boiled into a glue-like paste. Lowland communities often settle near groves of wild sago or plant it near their settlements.

Flying wide circles between the mountain walls that ringed the hidden paradise, we found a relatively flat valley floor that held an incredibly beautiful forest. Groves of ancient trees. Crystal-clear streams.

But no people.

Or dinosaurs, for that matter.

But I couldn't shake the feeling that this majestic place did hold mysteries. Almost ten years after those clear morning skies allowed us to fly the length of the valley, an expedition led by Conservation International hiked up into Dinosaur Valley and discovered numerous new species of birds, insects, mammals, marsupials, and reptiles living in this remote corner of God's wilderness.[7] If they found any T. rexes, they're not letting the rest of us in on it.

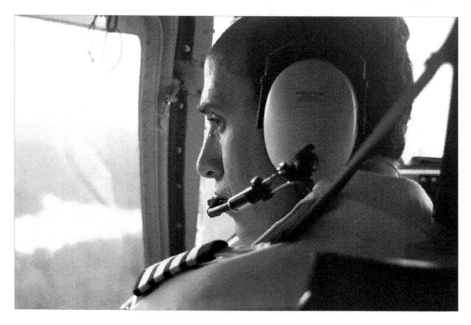

Nate looking out at Dinosaur Valley

Certain there were no people in Dinosaur Valley, we found the exit and flew farther westwards.

And there, in other valleys, we did find people.

At one point, we flew several miles up a tight canyon without seeing any traces of life. Up ahead a solid mountain wall signaled what I thought

7 See *National Geographic Magazine*, June 2010.

was the canyon's end. Through the clouds that hung over the ridgeline on my left, something caught my attention. I decided it was worth a second look, so I gently let the Helio descend 200 feet and made a second pass. Down lower, I could see that the thin clouds at the ridgeline concealed the narrow entrance into yet another valley, a bit like a long hall leading to a larger room. Peering through the translucent veil of mist, I could see the valley was shaped like a shallow bowl, where a solid layer of clouds gave it a roof of sorts. To get in, we'd have to slip through the narrow entrance. Once in we'd be trapped in the bowl, below the roof, with only one way out—the hallway we'd used to enter. It looked a little tight even for the Helio Courier's legendary low-speed maneuverability. And what would be the chances of anyone living up here in such isolation?

After a few more passes, which allowed me to evaluate the entrance of the valley, I knew that getting in and out of the valley was doable … and we couldn't leave this stone unturned. We went in.

Hooting and hollering on the intercom once again strained my ears. I think there were probably similar noises on the ground a few hundred feet below us. This hidden valley did indeed hold people. Tucked in a dense little grove of sago palms were a group of huts, which quickly emptied themselves of their occupants. The people on the ground stared at us for a while and then began waving enthusiastically up at the delighted linguists in the blue and white airplane circling overhead.

We don't really know, but it's possible that the people we found in that tiny valley had lived there completely isolated from the outside world, perhaps even unaware of the existence of neighboring tribal groups.

We carefully plotted the GPS position of every hamlet, hut, and garden that we found during the three days we spent following a multitude of river systems to their starting points deep in the mountains. Duane and Mark turned their data into a report that was used to help guide the next steps in the language survey process: the difficult task of putting survey teams on the ground to hike in overland and establish contact with the people groups we found and determine who they are and what languages they speak.

At the time of this book's publication, much survey has been done, but to the best of my knowledge, no one has made it up into that hidden valley in the Dark Triangle.

One of the tiny clusters of huts we spotted during our
survey flights over the Dark Triangle

4

WAHUKA HILL

Never pity missionaries; envy them. They are where the real action is—
where life and death, sin and grace, heaven and hell converge.
                                        —ROBERT C. SHANNON

A typical day at the end of the earth? Not sure there is such a thing. But let me tell you about yesterday.

I flip the switch on the coffee maker at 5:00 a.m. Sheri and our son, Cameron, are still sleeping soundly. At 5:30, I'm out the door. The sun is just beginning to brighten the skies to the east of Sentani, and the call to prayer echoes from the nearby mosque. My faithful, if rust-eaten, 1978 Landcruiser takes me the mile and a half to the airport on still-deserted roads.

I finish the preflight inspection* on UCA (*Uniform Charlie Alpha*), one of our four Helio Couriers, around 6:00. In the radio room, I get a good weather report from my destination, a tiny clearing in the jungle 200 nautical miles to the west called Foida. Walking back across the ramp to the airplane, the airport is coming to life—Cessna 206s, 185s, Caravans, Pilatus Porters, Antonovs, and Fokker F-27s are all starting up and taxiing out for their first flights of the day. Soon the Helio's engine adds its voice to the discordant chorus of pistons, turbines, jets, and propellers. At 6:36 a.m. the Helio breaks ground from the last piece of pavement it will see all day.

Today I'm headed for the mission station at Foida. Strapped under the cargo net are 800 pounds of supplies for the station. The Helio does a lot of things well, but at 120 knots, getting places quickly is not one of them. I have an hour and 45 minutes of nothing but trackless rainforest in front of me. Level at 6,000 feet, I nurse a cup of coffee and marvel at the splendor of what God has created here. A blanket of undisturbed jungle stretches as far as I can see. That vista is only broken when it meets majestic mountains on the horizon. Topping out at 16,000 feet, the ragged peaks are beautiful, even peaceful, in the clear early morning air. By 9:00 they will be shrouded in building clouds.

At 7:00 I call Foida to double-check the weather. The initial report I received before leaving Sentani is proving to have been optimistic. The trees of this vast section of rainforest have their roots in a swamp that covers thousands of square miles, and, as is common, a fog has formed right after sunrise. I'm still an hour and twenty minutes out, and typically the fog will lift by 8:30, so for now, I keep UCA's nose pointed west.

Thirty miles out of Foida, small holes and creases begin to appear in the undercast. I can see the serpentine Rouffaer River through the breaks. Ten miles out I choose a break in the clouds that's right above a bend in the river and slow the airplane down. Now this is something the Helio does wonderfully: slow, safe, controllable flight. With full flaps and 50 knots of airspeed, I'm still 20 knots above the stall speed. Getting through the hole is tight but wouldn't even be a reasonably safe proposition in other fixed wing aircraft.

Now I'm under the clouds, 400 feet above the river, with 30 miles visibility in all directions. I follow the river around a few bends until the airstrip at Foida comes into view. The Helio makes short work of the approach to the 1,200-foot strip, and soon I'm shutting down. It's 8:30.

I'm greeted by enthusiastic members of the Kirikiri tribe. "Bokobara!" they fairly shout as they grab my hand. They're even friendlier than usual, perhaps because I'm planning to visit their village of Wahuka today. After securing the aircraft, I walk with the Kirikiri down to the river's edge. As I'm getting into the 40-foot dugout canoe to go downriver, it dawns on me that every single man is armed with his bow and arrows. That's a bit unusual. I mention this to Jerry, the mission worker, as he starts the canoe's outboard motor. He explains that one fellow in the canoe has an enemy who has sworn to ambush him—thus the armed escort.

As we make our way downriver, the canoe's passing flushes flocks of cockatoos, parrots, and hornbills into flight—glorious reminders of the creative passion of the One who made this place. One tree on the right bank, standing taller than the rest, catches my attention. Several hundred enormous fruit bats hang from its branches, while at least that many circle the tree in a chaotic holding pattern. Most of them have wing spans of over 4 feet.

Halfway to Wahuka, we pass the hut of our passenger's enemy. The Kirikiri in the boat exchange shouts with the man on the shore. It's probably a good thing I don't understand Kirikiri. I've got a feeling the vocabulary in this exchange wasn't stuff you'd pick up in Sunday school.

We beach the canoe at the base of Wahuka Hill. It takes all the dexterity I can muster to exit the canoe without getting wet. Alas, staying dry was to be a short-lived state of affairs—the getting-wet part happens as we trek through the short stretch of swamp that leads to the base of the hill. Logs have been laid into the bog with the purpose, I can only assume, of allowing one to walk through the swamp without getting one's feet wet. Unfortunately, most of the logs are awash in six inches of swamp. I abandon any hopes of not having soggy boots today.

Eventually my soaked boots leave the swamp behind, and the trail begins to wind up a steep incline. When we emerge from the jungle, we are at the top of Wahuka Hill. This small bump of a hill is an anomaly in the vastness of the flat swamp that surrounds it. The crest has been transformed from a dense forest into a hard, steeply sloped clearing of red earth. This is what I've come to see. This stretch of dirt had no significance except that we were hoping to one day land an airplane on it. A future airstrip.

Almost four years had passed since I first walked this hill with Duane Clouse. Duane and his wife, Helja, dedicated their lives to serving the Kirikiri people. Wahuka Hill is the only terrain in the Kirikiri territory that doesn't flood when the river gets high, thus the only place to put an airstrip. Our Helio Couriers have been the Clouses' only means of reaching the Kirikiri, but until now, we've only been able to get them

Duane Clouse with Kirikiri friends

"almost there." They've always had to finish the journey with the sometimes-hazardous canoe trip I've just taken.

When I first walked the hill with Duane, we were trying to determine if putting an airstrip on this tiny hill was even possible. At the end of that day's work, the answer was: "yes … just barely." After four years of back-breaking labor—imagine completely redefining the profile of a hill, moving thousands of cubic yards of dirt and rock, all by hand, I'm once again carrying a measuring tape and inclinometer to Wahuka Hill. But today, my purpose is to evaluate whether the airstrip meets our specifications and is actually safe to land on.

The best way to get a picture of this airstrip is to imagine standing at the bottom of a ski slope in the middle of summer. (If you want the full Wahuka experience, drag a portable sauna to the ski slope, fill it with a couple of thousand flies with ADHD, set the temp to "Beastly Hot," and jump in.) The short touchdown zone has a 10% slope that quickly

The completed Wahuka airstrip just prior to the first landing

increases to 17%. The entire strip is less than 1,000 feet long. Because of the shape of the hill, you can't see the top from the bottom and vice versa.

The airstrip has significant drainage problems, but with a little work they can be corrected. I gather the Kirikiri around and give them a pep talk about finishing well. To encourage them in their work, I tell them that I plan to make a test landing today, which elicits hoots, hollers, and lots of smiles.

Back down the hill, through the swamp, into the canoe, and back upriver to Foida. We stop along the way for one of the passengers in the canoe to haul in a huge river turtle he has caught—2½ feet long, nose to tail.

The short flight from Foida passes quickly, and soon I'm overhead Wahuka. On the first approach, I plan to make a low pass—just to get a feel for the right altitudes, approach path, and committal point.

On short final I veer off to the right. Things feel really good. Time for the real thing. Integrity requires that I dispense with any notions that I'm an ice-cool bush pilot; I was nervous. A first landing anywhere is an endeavor with heightened risk, and on a strip this short, with this much slope change, my inner scaredy-cat was making more noise than I'd like to admit. Even though I thought I was prepared for it, the way the airstrip rushes up at me in the last seconds before touchdown takes my breath away. I hang on, and somehow the landing works itself out.

On short final to Wahuka. This tiny hillock in the middle of a vast swamp was transformed (by hand!) into a runway—a portal for reaching the Kiri-Kiri people. (Photo courtesy of Glenn Grubb)

What a feeling to land an airplane on an airstrip for the very first time, especially one that I'd had the privilege of watching evolve from a forest-covered hill to rugged strip. I shut down at the top of the strip. Instead of the jubilant dancing I anticipated, there is only silence. I climb out of the Helio and realize that the people are only obeying to the letter my instructions that no one be on the airstrip while I'm landing. I yell "Bokobara!" and absolute mayhem is unleashed. The people whoop, shout, and dance in celebration. They surround the airplane, a mass of people jumping up and down in unison, yelling at the top of their lungs. What a moment! Eventually, things calm down, and we gather under the wing and pray. A young Kirikiri fellow named Simon, who knows the trade language, translates my prayer. It's 12:30.

Takeoff down the hill is exhilarating, but I'm far more relaxed than I was for the landing. Once again, I head back to Foida, this time to pick up three passengers bound for Sentani. Three passengers? Make that nine, if you include the six large (and very much alive) river turtles they loaded in the cargo pod among their bags. It's 1:25.

I don't have enough fuel to make a direct flight home, so we head to Lake Holmes. Sixty miles from Foida, we stock fuel in drums at this lakeside airstrip. The weather at the lake is a bit grumpy, but it's one of the few airstrips we can land on with light rain on the windshield. It's 2:00. My friends Weinus and Wewur help out by pumping 20 gallons of avgas out of a drum into the wings. The people at Lake Holmes want to send some fish out on the airplane. I open the cargo pod to find dozens of fat, greasy sago grubs doing their squirm thing in between all the other baggage. Somebody didn't secure their container adequately. Oh well, they're not going anywhere. In go the fish. They join the grubs and the turtles. A flying smorgasbord. Soon we're airborne again, picking our way around the rain showers for the 170-mile trip home.

At 3:30 the Helio is back on the same parking spot that we left from this morning. I pull off my helmet for the last time today and slide out of the seat. I'm tired, but, as I often feel at the end of a day, grateful to be a part of what God is doing to reach the isolated peoples of this incredible land.

***

Several months later I found myself once again on short final to that steep clearing on the side of Wahuka Hill. This time I had the Clouses with me.

Duane and Helja stepped out of the Helio … and into their front yard. For the first time in the fifteen years they have been working among the Kirikiri, there is no waiting for the canoe, no precarious loading of the tipsy craft, no 45-minute river trip praying that it doesn't rain, the engine doesn't quit, catch fire, or fall off (all of which had happened). No hauling their gear and selves up the slippery trail to the top of Wahuka Hill. No, today, it's 25 paces to the house, unpack, eat lunch, and right to work. Or so I thought.

Immediately upon shutdown, the airplane was thronged with Kirikiri. They whisked Duane out the door—his feet never touched the ground— and carried him in a deafening, joyous procession around the airplane, whooping, hollering, and dancing as only the Kirikiri do. Helja was soon caught up in the same happy melee. She was desperately trying to video Duane's wild ride on the sea of hands, but the women lifting her up and down were rendering her best attempts futile. Reaching across the crowd, I grabbed Helja's video camera and filmed the wild scene for her.

How poignant that the first passengers to arrive at the new Wahuka airstrip were the people who have committed their lives to bringing light into the Kirikiri darkness. The significance was obviously not lost on the Kirikiri themselves.

The first passengers out of Wahuka? A little girl bitten by a poisonous snake and her mom.

5

BEACH TRIP

I never made a sacrifice.
—David Livingstone

I don't normally get to go to the beach on work time, but this was an unusual week from start to finish. With a light flight schedule, I was anticipating being able to devote a lot of time to some training and a few office projects.

Not to be. It all started with a phone call early Monday morning.

A new family had just moved to the coastal village of Arbais, 140 miles west of Sentani. From South Africa, Andy and Debbie Abbott came with a passion to accelerate the literacy program among the Isirawa people in preparation for their receiving the New Testament in a few short years.

We could fly the Abbotts to a runway on the coast about 30 miles from Arbais. From there the remainder of the journey was difficult and dangerous in a small boat on the open ocean. There actually was an airstrip at Arbais, but it hadn't been used in twenty years—in the tropics, the green stuff gets pretty thick in twenty years. The Abbotts and the Isirawa were working to clear overgrown runway and make it usable again.

Over the weekend, their infant daughter, Jessie, became very ill with malaria. There were times during the night on Sunday when they thought they were going to lose her. With a long boat trip on heavy seas out of the question and the airstrip not yet usable, it appeared as though the Abbotts were stranded far from medical help. There was one other option: land an aircraft on the beach.

I was airborne early Monday morning, following the coast for the 135 nautical miles to Arbais, hoping to arrive before the sea breeze picked up. Arriving over the tiny coastal village, I was relieved to see that the tide was out. Andy had marked out a clear section of sand with banana leaves. At my request, he'd also lit a fire so that the smoke would serve as a wind indicator. As I circled, the smoke from Andy's fire went straight up: the wind was perfectly calm.

So far, things were falling into place nicely. I did a low pass and rolled the wheels on the beach to check the surface condition of the sand. It felt smooth and solid. I came around to line up on the beach for real.

Landing the Helio Courier on the beach at Arbais

At touchdown, I was instantly impressed with the firmness and smoothness of the beach surface. Best airstrip surface in all of Papua, by far. Unfortunately, that beautiful surface would be gone a few hours later when the tide came in.

It was my first beach landing, and quite likely my last. We were able to get the Abbotts safely out that day, and Jessie recovered just fine. A study in perseverance, Andy and Debbie returned to Arbais many times.

The airstrip was eventually finished and many Isirawa learned to read and write in their own language. Years after that sleepless night of praying over Jessie, it all paid off.

Now I can understand the Scriptures!

The voices of the Isirawa people echoed this theme as they celebrated receiving the New Testament in their language. It had been five years since that beach landing in Arbais. Jessie was now an active seven-year-old scampering around the dedication activities with her Isirawa friends. I well remember the weariness and discouragement on Jessie's parents' faces that morning on the beach. What hope we would all have had that day had we been able to fast forward and see their faces transformed by the joy I saw in them on Dedication Day.

Dedication Day in Arbais. Isirawa children read the Scriptures in their own language for the first time. (Photographer unknown)

On that happy day of celebration, we used four aircraft to shuttle over fifty people in and out of Arbais. The rehabilitated airstrip performed flawlessly.

I'm still partial to landing on the beach.

6

ISAAK

The journey doesn't end here.
Death is just another path, one that we all must take.
—Gandalf to Pippen in the battle of Minas Tirith in The Lord of the Rings

I sometimes think about the stories our aircraft would tell if they could. Some of our Helios started their service lives in war-torn Southeast Asia. A few have sheet metal patches that suggest bullet holes. What a road they've traveled to end up in Papua.

I suppose these planes would talk about the places they'd been. The mountain passes they'd navigated. The oceans they'd crossed. The close calls with bad weather, low fuel, high trees. The touch of the different pilots. The different paint jobs they'd worn over the years…

I think most interesting to me would be the stories of the passengers and cargo these faithful aircraft have carried. Young missionary families full of apprehension, dreams, and enthusiasm on their way to their first village assignment. Exhausted veterans of the struggle in the jungle, climbing on board, their battle-tested dreams still intact, but showing signs of wear. A day-old baby. An old man heading back to his village to die. Ordinary people. High government officials. Christians. Animists. Muslims. Adventurers looking for their Shangri-la's. Translated portions of God's Word. Mail. Money. Pigs. Cats. Cows. Crocs. Tree kangaroos. Rice. Cement. Tin roofing. Toilets. Plywood. Sinks. Isaak.

Let me tell you about Isaak.

Few things are louder than a Helio engine, but on this day, long before the prop stopped spinning, I could hear the wailing of the Bauzis. I'd just landed at Noiadi, the Bauzi village where Dave and Joyce Briley were working to translate the Scriptures. I had Isaak with me in the back.

That's wrong. Isaak was in a much better place than the back of a Helio. His body, however, was strapped to the floor of the airplane.

The aircraft was immediately surrounded by a throng of Bauzis. I could hardly open my door. The noise was absolutely deafening. My culture mourns staid and composed, rarely showing the pain we throttle inside our souls. The Bauzis mourn with unfettered abandon. Picture fifty people pressing in around you, anguishing at the top of their lungs. Their gut-wrenching, soul-rending grief reverberated throughout the still air of the entire river valley. I slipped through the crowd to the back of the airplane. As I leaned on the tail, enveloped in this unbelievable scene, my own tears started. In the sea of brown faces a white one caught my eye. I moved over next to Dave. His tears flowed freely.

"I don't know what I'm going to do without him. He was my right hand." Looking down at the women draped over Isaak's unmoving frame, Dave choked out, "He was about the only one that really had a vision for the Word."

Isaak was indeed Dave's right hand. Together they worked long hours searching for the right words to convey the transforming truths of God's Word in the Bauzi language. From a human perspective, this was a huge setback in reaching this particular corner of the end of the earth.

A few weeks earlier, one of our pilots had strapped Isaak's still-breathing body into the airplane to take him out to the coast. He was sick, and no medicine in the village seemed to help. No medicine at the hospital seemed to help either, and before long he stepped into the presence of Jesus. Now he was to be buried back in Noiadi.

As his body was committed to the ground, many joined the Brileys in asking God to raise up more Isaaks from among the Bauzis to take up the task that will ultimately lead their tribe to freedom.

7

SIGNIFICANT ENDEAVORS

There is no defeat unless one loses God, and then all is defeat,
though it be housed in castles and buried in fortunes.
—FRANK LAUBACH

Dave gave up. His head swimming in a malarial blur, he stumbled away from the HF radio and headed back to bed. He made a few steps in that direction and passed out, collapsing to the floor.

The radio crackled to life.

YAJASI 275 standing by for emergency radio traffic.

For most pilots, flying is fun, and we can't believe we get paid to do this job (I think I may have just lost my union card). We take the weekend off only because we have to and because the real heroes of our operation, the mechanics, deserve a break. But just in case somebody needs to call the Jungle 911, the pilots take turns being on standby for the weekend. Other staff members (alas, the mechanics have to take their turn too) rotate through radio standby, coming up on the HF radio at three regularly scheduled times during the day on weekends.[8]

At four o'clock in the afternoon on this particular Saturday, Mike Bucklin, our chief of maintenance, had come into the hangar to do the last emergency standby radio schedule for the day.

---

8 With the advent of affordable satellite phones, we have since discontinued this practice.

One hundred and sixty nautical miles to the west, Dave Briley lay prone on the bark floor of the village radio shack, his sweat-soaked shirt clammy against his skin. With his family back on the coast, Dave was alone in the Bauzi village of Noiadi, working hard on translating the book of Romans. He'd been feeling lousy for a couple of days and recognized the all-too-familiar symptoms of malaria. Now the disease had taken a nasty turn, and he knew it was time to get out of Noiadi. Though weak, he'd managed to make it to the radio shack a few dozen paces from his house. After a couple of calls went unanswered, he started to stumble back towards his bed and ended up in harmony with the floor.

Dave Briley working on the Bauzi translation in Noiadi
(Photo courtesy of Tim Harold)

Then came Mike's call.

YAJASI 275 standing by for emergency radio traffic.

Of course, Dave didn't hear Mike's call. But a Bauzi man did. He grabbed the microphone. In broken Indonesian he explained the situation.

On the other end, Mike picked up the phone and called the pilot on standby for the weekend … which happened to be me. Unfortunately, there was nothing we could do right away: it was too late in the day to make it to Noiadi before dark. Dave would have to hang on until the following morning.

I hung up the phone and thought back to my last flight into Noiadi. I had brought Isaak, the key Bauzi on the translation project, back to his village to be buried. Now Dave was seriously ill.

Every significant endeavor encounters significant opposition.

Sunday morning found me 600 feet above the Noiadi canyon floor, just below the ridgeline, following the river to the 1,000-foot-long airstrip.

I found Dave lying on the bark-floored side porch of his simple wood-plank home, surrounded by concerned Bauzis. Normally a rowdy, fun-loving bunch, the Bauzis were subdued. I could read the fear on their faces: Were they going to lose Dave just as they had lost Isaak? An animistic worldview would have had them wondering if the forces of darkness were gaining the upper hand.

A Bauzi man and I helped keep Dave vertical as we walked him to the airstrip. "Thanks for coming," Dave mumbled. "Last night was terrible. I really didn't think I was going to make it."

Soon Dave was lying down in the back of the Helio with an oxygen mask obscuring his features. I prayed for him. All the Bauzi heads were lowered, bows and arrows held still. The believers among them joined in earnestly.

Then we were off. With a string of recent tragedies, I'm sure that as the Bauzis listened to the Helio's roar slowly fade into the distance, they wondered if they'd ever see Dave again.

Dave was indeed very sick. Malaria can be a very stubborn thing. It can be a deadly thing. Praise God, Dave did recover, but I think it was almost a month before he was completely well.

And the Bauzi guy who answered the radio that afternoon while Dave lay in a heap on the floor? Same guy who helped me get Dave to the

Rudy's work on the New Testament translation helped bring salvation to his people. He's pictured here several years after the events of this story, after the Scriptures in Bauzi had been published. Rudy's call on the radio saved Dave Briley's life.
(Photo courtesy of Tim Harold)

airplane. His name was Rudy. He's the man that God raised up to replace Isaak. That day in the radio shack, he helped save Dave's life.

Shortly after he was back on his feet, Dave spoke these words:

Five more books and we'll be done with the Bauzi New Testament. What keeps me at this task is that even while we're working at the table figuring out the translation, day by day God is working out salvation in the lives of these people. He's taken away their hearts of stone and given them hearts of flesh.

In March 2009, all the blood, sweat, and tears paid off, and the prayers of many were answered. As it had on the day I brought Isaak's body home, the Noiadi valley once again reverberated with a multitude of Bauzi voices. Now they celebrated life: the arrival of the Scriptures in their own language.

Isaak had the best seat in the house.

8

A NEW LIFE'S FIRST FLIGHT

I am a missionary, heart and soul. God had an only Son, and
he was a missionary and a physician. A poor, poor imitation I am
or wish to be. In this service I hope to live; in it I wish to die.
—DAVID LIVINGSTONE

I ran into Margreet Kroneman on my way home from the hangar today.

"Nate, I hear you're delivering babies in flight. What next!"

Good to see that the jungle grapevine was working as per normal: fast and wrong. I had to tell Margreet that things didn't quite transpire like she'd heard.

It was one of those little pop-up medical emergencies that happen quite frequently while flying in Papua. I was en route to my first stop of the day. The guy on the radio was saying that a woman had delivered the night before, the baby was fine, but the mother had retained the placenta. I asked if they needed me to drop what I was doing and come right away. The guy tells me that mom and baby were both doing fine and that getting there after my morning's scheduled flying would be great. I told them I could do that, and I'd be there by late morning. Actually, this fit nicely into my schedule for the day: a run to three villages to pick up pastors and deliver them to a central spot for a church conference, and then I was scheduled to be empty on the homebound leg. Neat and tidy, just the way I like my emergencies.

The church-conference flying came off pretty much as planned, and around 11:00 a.m. I found myself touching down on the short airstrip at Gidoman. I had one other passenger with me, a noncritical patient from one of my earlier stops, who just happened to be from the same language group as those in Gidoman. On this day, as it turned out, none of those who had turned up at the airstrip spoke any Indonesian (this place is pretty well off the beaten track, lots of gourds and grass skirts). Fortunately, my passenger, the sick guy, spoke Indonesian quite well, and I was able to use him as an interpreter.

Me: "How's the woman?"

Them: "OK."

Me: "How's the baby?"

Them: "Fine."

Me: "Can the woman sit in a seat or does she need to lie down?"

Them: "She needs to lie down."

I began removing seats and configuring the airplane for the patient. As I was busy doing my thing, I noticed they had laid her next to the airplane on a makeshift stretcher. Fabric being a premium in these parts, the only "clothing" she had was a dirty rice sack draped across her waist. Modesty was preserved, but only just. I figured they'd bring the baby to the airplane after the mother was strapped in.

We pulled the poles out of her "stretcher" (more rice sacks), and four of us lifted her into the airplane. I hadn't really noticed her face until this point … she was but a lass, perhaps sixteen. As I began to pull the end of my cargo net up to drape over her legs, she reached down and lifted up the rice sack, revealing a bloodied grass skirt and … a baby boy. My heart did one of those cold stops it normally saves for the times when it thinks that what's about to happen can no longer be considered a "landing." How she hid this little one under that sack I'll never know. Apparently, the baby's arm had gotten twisted in all of our gymnastics getting her into the airplane, and she felt the need to rearrange the little guy.

Me: "Hey! She's got the baby down here!"

Them: "Yeah, we can't cut the cord because she hasn't birthed the placenta yet, and if we cut the cord she'll die."[9]

9 Apparently, this belief is fairly common in the interior of Papua.

Me: "Well, let's put the little guy up on her tummy so he can nurse during the flight."

Them: "Can't. The cord's too short."

Me: "When was the baby born?"

Them: "Yesterday."

Me: "And he hasn't nursed yet?"

Them: "Can't. We told you already: the cord's too short."

Me: "Uuooh boy."

Now I'm moving fast. The baby's color looks good. The girl's temp feels good. Pulse very fast … the baby's was too, but I think I remember that being normal for newborns. I'm thinking about how I've heard doctors stress the importance of getting nutrition into a newborn right away after birth. For a moment, I contemplate cutting the cord with the little scissors on my Swiss Army knife. Then calmer thoughts prevail. Thoughts like: I'm 45 minutes away from medical competence, let them do it.

I thank the Lord I have my oxygen bottle with me today. Through my interpreter, I explain to the mother to breathe normally even with the mask over her face. Though she makes no noise, tears flow down her cheeks as I pull the mask over her mouth and nose. Her eyes speak her fear. I tell my interpreter, "Tell her this will help her and her baby to live." He does, and it seems to calm her.

I pray in Indonesian. Might as well have been in English. God and the interpreter are the only ones present that understand.

A quick shot of avgas out of the wings cleans the blood off my hands, then it's into the cockpit and we're off. For the sake of the patients, we fly low, following the rivers out of the foothills and then stay below 3,000 feet all the way home. I call ahead to have a nurse ready to cut the cord and get this guy nursing right after we land. Home base wants to relay some questions from the nurse:

"Is she bleeding?"

I glance at the stains on my clothes from lifting her into the airplane. "Yeah."

After arrival in Sentani they took her to a nearby clinic. On my way to work the next morning I stopped in. Much to my delight, mother and little one were doing wonderfully. Neither I nor the nurse could communicate with her due to the language barrier, so we just exchanged smiles.

As I left, I glanced back through the open door. I have a picture imprinted in my mind's eye of this girl, whose name I never learned, twisting in her bed to watch me leave. The look on her face still moves me to tears as I write this. Not a single word. I don't understand a single word of her language, but her expression conveyed something that, with all the words of English available to me, I find difficult to describe. The closest I can get is to describe its effect on me: the look on her face is one of the things that will keep bringing me back to Papua.

9

To Go in Peace

Perfect love drives out fear.
—John the Apostle

I had five passengers and two stops to make. I'd just landed at an airstrip in Fayu territory to drop off three of the passengers. The plan was then to take the other two, a young Elopi couple, on to their village 15 miles away.

I swung out of the seat and dropped down to the muddy airstrip below. As I've done perhaps a thousand times, my hand automatically reached up through the open pilot's door to the rear door latch. My hand finds the familiar handle, but before I can open the door another hand clamps itself firmly on top of mine. Someone doesn't want this door open.

"What's the matter?" I ask, leaning into the airplane.

"I'm *scared*. I'm not getting out of the airplane," came the response. The voice belonged to the Elopi man I was to drop at the next village. It dawned on me that historically the Elopi and the Fayu had done their level best to wipe each other out. A recent ambush had left three men dead. The thirty Fayu men standing along the edge of the airstrip, armed to the teeth with bows and arrows and spears, probably didn't help much.

I assured my Elopi friend that these people weren't party to the warfare; they were armed for self-defense … or hunting perhaps? These Fayu, I promised, were friendly and wouldn't hurt him or his wife. I even gave

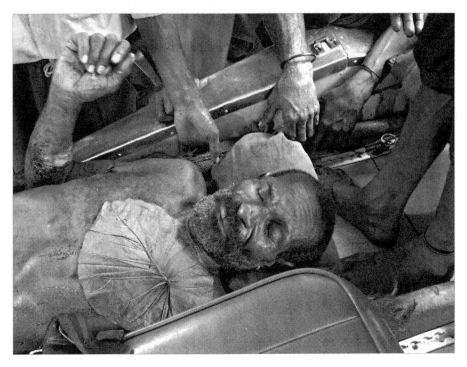

Medevac flight for a man injured in tribal
warfare in the Fayu/Elopi area

him my personal guarantee of his safety. No dice. His hand remained firmly clamped on mine preventing me from opening the door.

OK, you can wait in the airplane and roast if you want. Twenty minutes past noon, 200 feet above sea level, 4 degrees below the equator, 45 degrees above comfortable, and you and your bride want to stay in the greenhouse-like Helio? Suit yourself.

I went about my business, the first order of which was extracting my other passengers from the airplane—they were seated in the very rear row of seats and actually had to climb over the immovable couple to exit the aircraft. I then began to unload the cargo pod*.

As per usual, the people from the Fayu community began crowding around the airplane. I noticed several talking through the windows to the man and his wife. Because the Fayu and Elopi languages are mutually unintelligible, they had to use Indonesian, which meant I could understand the conversation.

The Fayu were attempting to convince our man that they were friendly. They extended their arms through the still-open pilot door to offer him a handshake. The man refused their overtures, keeping both hands firmly clenched on the rear door latch. No one was going to open that door. Pulling cargo out of the pod, I kept a close eye on the proceedings. Despite the confident voice of my own assurances, I wasn't 100 percent convinced myself of the Fayus' peaceful intentions. The Fayus kept repeating a phrase. I had to listen closely to catch it:

Don't worry, we have Jesus now.

The next thing I know, the door is open, and our passenger is now walking towards the jungle at the edge of the airstrip, hand in hand with his erstwhile enemy. This caused me no small degree of alarm. Treachery is a highly esteemed character trait in these parts, using friendliness to break down a victim's guard before moving in for the kill. I jumped in with a query as to what was going on. It turns out our Elopi passenger had a very real need to visit the "little boys' room" (which, in the Papuan context, is any part of the jungle not currently being used as a little girls' room). The Fayu man at the airplane's door had guaranteed the Elopi passenger's safety and would hold his hand for the entire time he was out of the airplane as a sign of that guarantee.

Greater love has no man …
than to hold the hand of an enemy so that he can "go in peace."

Building this airstrip by hand, in the middle of the jungle, was a five-year herculean feat. For that matter, everything about reaching the isolated peoples of Papua consumes an enormous amount of time, money, and effort. Why bother?

Don't worry, we have Jesus now.

That's why.

10

WHAT A DAY CAN HOLD

Let us touch the dying.
—MOTHER TERESA

Four-year-olds and their questions.

"Daddy, what does 'die' mean?" my son, Cameron, asked me the other day. "Cameron," I responded, "you will always be. Dying is just when your body stops working."

A few days later I had cause to remember those words.

As usual, the radio frequency for communicating with the interior airstrips is a zoo this morning. Through all the chatter, I finally get through to my destination to ask for a weather report. "Clear," comes the response, which I know from experience to mean anything from *not a cloud in the sky* to just short of *fire and brimstone*. Ah well, I'll probably get in. After the succinct weather report, they ask if I can take a critical patient to Wamena, the central hub of the highlands. Can do.

The airstrip at Kanggime is nestled in a tight valley 4,500 feet above sea level. After the hour-and-twenty-minute flight from Sentani, we're soon unloading the missionary and his cargo at the end of the airstrip. I ask to see the patient.

In a nearby hut, an old Dani tribesman is curled up on a jungle stretcher made of woven pandanus fronds strung between two poles. Clumps of moss are packed beneath him to give him a bit of a mattress.

The people's diagnosis: malaria. The two Dani men who plan to accompany the patient to Wamena help me lay him in the back of the Helio Courier. Minutes later we are snaking our way through the mountain passes that lead us into the expansive Baliem Valley. We fly the length of the valley and at the east end line up for an approach to Wamena's airport. I've radioed ahead to have transportation ready from the hospital.

On the ground, I'm greeted by the staff from Helimission, good friends and partners in ministry. Since the hospital can't send an ambulance, Helimission graciously provides their car. With the small van backed up to the airplane, I jump inside the cabin of the airplane to assist moving the patient to the vehicle. The two Dani passengers help.

As I cradle his head, something doesn't seem right. I feel for a pulse. Nothing. I rip open his shirt to look for signs of breathing. Nothing. I put my hand over his mouth and nose to feel for breath. Nothing. He's gone.

In the cramped quarters of the back of the van, I'm huddled over a man who started life in a grass hut and finished it in an airplane. The other Dani man in the van with me is looking at me, his eyes full of question. "He's dead," I say. "Are you related to him?"

"He's my father," he says, tears welling in his eyes.

"Did he know Jesus?" I ask.

"Yes." I take off my sweaty baseball cap and we bow our heads. Together we thank God for eternal life and commit this old Dani man into the hands of his Maker.

"Papua," says one of the Helimission mechanics as the van pulls away, "you never know what a day will hold." We stand there, sobered, stilled.

As we stood next to the airplane, watching the van pull away, 300 miles to our west, two other Helio Couriers were winging their way towards the far western edge of the Birds Head region of Papua. On this five-day trip they will provide the air transportation necessary for the dedication and celebration of the newly translated Scriptures in the Abun language. For the Abun people, this day holds life. May they take hold of that life and gain the same hope of the Dani man whose body stopped working in my Helio this morning.

11

REUNIONS

The proper function of man is to live, not to exist.
—JACK LONDON

One of my earliest memories of flying is of sitting on my dad's lap in the front passenger seat of a Pilatus Porter, watching the Himalayas go by, with Everest, a mysterious dark peak, in the far distance.

The other day, as I watched a different set of mountains go by, I thought about how life sometimes comes full circle. My interest in aviation was birthed in a Porter. Thirty years later I find myself at the controls of this amazing aircraft.

For many of us at YAJASI, the thought of putting our Helio Couriers out to pasture felt like turning your back on your best friend. Since 1976, these amazing short-takeoff-and-landing (STOL) aircraft have served the Bible translation movement in Papua. The brainchild of Otto Koppen, a professor of aeronautical engineering at the Massachusetts Institute of Technology, the Helio was designed from the ground up to do STOL like no other aircraft had ever done. When the first Helio came off the production line in 1954, its leading-edge slats, huge flaps, and interceptors allowed the aircraft to fly stabilized approaches at 50 knots. Its rugged landing gear and tubular steel frame were built specifically to handle the abuse that remote airstrips would dish out ... and many consider it the most crashworthy aircraft ever built.

The development of the Helio had an immediate impact on Bible translation. Wycliffe Bible Translators' founder, William Cameron Townsend, happened to see a Helio land in an open field, using only a few hundred feet to get stopped. He knew then and there that he'd found the perfect airplane to help his teams reach isolated communities with the Word of God. And the airplane has done just that, and done it well. Since JAARS[10] took delivery of their first Helio in 1955, serial number 22, the aircraft have been used all over the world to speed the work of Bible translation and to minister to isolated and often marginalized minority communities. By any measure, a term of service that exceeds fifty years is a fantastic record for an aircraft type.

In the early years, Nate flew the Helio Courier in the service of reaching the isolated people groups of Papua. He thoroughly enjoyed the privilege of flying this remarkable aircraft.

But an era, by definition, has a beginning and an end. Our Helios serving in Papua were built in the late 1960s; they are older than many of

10 Townsend founded JAARS as the Jungle Aviation and Radio Service in 1948 to provide aviation and communications support for the work of Bible translation in remote parts of the world. Since 1961 JAARS has been headquartered at its center in Waxhaw, North Carolina.

the guys flying them. The Helio factory has been closed since 1974, and getting parts for these old birds was becoming increasingly difficult. The kicker was fuel: the piston engines that power the Helios run on aviation gasoline (avgas). Avgas is not produced in Indonesia, and importing the fuel from outside the country was becoming increasingly difficult. When we could get it, avgas cost us as much as $12 per gallon. The writing was on the wall, and we all knew it: we couldn't continue to support the Bible translation movement in Papua with the aging avgas-burning Helios. With more than one hundred people groups still waiting for a translation of the Scriptures into their languages, we knew we needed to find another STOL aircraft—a current, in-production airplane that ran on readily available, reasonably priced jet fuel. We evaluated a number of aircraft, but, in the end, the Swiss-made Pilatus Porter was an easy choice. Using a Pratt and Whitney turboprop engine that burns jet fuel, the Porter carries more than twice the payload of the Helio and yet has the STOL performance to operate on the same short, rough airstrips.

In time, God provided us with four of these $1.7 million aircraft—all of them given to us by members of the body of Christ in an amazing display of their passion to use their resources to reach some of the most isolated people on the planet.

And so, I find myself this morning in the front office of a Pilatus Porter watching the snowcapped peaks of Papua's western highlands slide by. I'm en route to Bugalaga, perhaps the perfect name for a jungle airstrip. Perched 6,000 feet above sea level, this mountain airstrip has served the people of the area since the 1970s. For today's mission, Bugalaga will serve as a rendezvous point, as well as facilitate a couple of reunions.

It's my first time in to Bugalaga, so I'm grateful for this morning's calm conditions and clear weather. The airstrip has a reputation for treacherous winds and turbulence. On final approach, my peripheral vision catches a graphic reminder of what the wind can do to the unwary pilot.

After landing, the people are super, and many helping hands unload the 1,650 pounds of cargo from my airplane. I wander over to a pile of wreckage at the side of the airstrip. It's a Pilatus Porter, the abandoned airframe still maintaining an air of dignity as it lies peacefully in the weeds.

We meet again, old friend.

Improbable as it seems, this is the very airplane in which I flew as a child in Nepal. When the JAARS aviation program in Nepal closed in the mid-seventies, the Porter was sold and spent the next two decades in Europe. The aircraft was then purchased by a commercial operator in Papua, only to end up in a heap at the end of the airstrip at Bugalaga.

Poking around the wreckage, I run into some interesting bits and pieces ... and a rustling in my soul that feels something like homesickness. This aluminum fuselage is a piece of my personal history, a link to Bohkraha, Biratnagar, and Kathmandu, my childhood locales to which I'd never returned.

Reuniting with the aircraft where it all began for Nate. Riding in this aircraft as a child in Nepal sparked his early interest in aviation.

Nostalgia's spell is broken by the distant sound of another airplane approaching the valley. A second Porter, flown by Syd Johnsen, is soon touching down on the steeply sloped airstrip. Missionaries Rich and Karen Brown are Syd's passengers, their three little girls' faces plastered to the windows as he pulls in to park next to my airplane (which carried the Browns' cargo).

Not much later, there is a growing rumble in the valley again: the distinctive sound of a helicopter echoing off the ridges. Since the airstrip at Daboto isn't finished, Syd and I have rendezvoused with the helicopter here in Bugalaga. The heli will fly a number of shuttles to move the Browns into their new assignment of loving the Moi.

It's been five years since those first memorable experiences in X-Ray. Since today is a day of reunions, it's fitting that it's the same helicopter and the same pilot as on that first trip into the X-Ray valley.

Always good to see Brian.

12

THE LONG SIT

God's work done in God's way will never lack God's supply.
—HUDSON TAYLOR

Looking at the waves 13,000 feet below us, I wiggled in my seat and thought, *You'd think that in an airplane this expensive they could make a comfortable seat.* The day wasn't even half over, and I'd already spent over four hours sitting in the Pilatus Porter's padding-deficient seat. For all of its strengths, no one would ever accuse the Pilatus Porter of being fast or comfortable. Perhaps that's one of the reasons the Porter is sometimes called the jeep of the air.

We were crossing the 60-mile stretch of open ocean between the mainland of Papua and the Aru Island group of the Maluku Province. At the controls of the airplane, Brad McFarlane suffered in his equally uncomfortable seat. I sat in the back squished up against the cumbersome bundle of a life raft. The rest of the cabin was filled with members of the Aru team: a group of missionaries working together to translate the Bible into the four different languages of the Aru Islands. For the next 15 minutes we would be out of gliding distance from land … meaning that if our reliable engine decided to become unreliable, we'd all be getting wet. Thus, the raft and my short-straw duty to man it.

At the end of the 12-hour day, Brad and I had traveled 1,000 nautical miles and spent over 8 hours in those tortuous seats, pushing our jeep of the air into a role it wasn't designed for. Right mission, wrong tool.

It was exactly because of these types of missions that we began asking God to provide us with a Pilatus PC-12 aircraft. This high-speed, pressurized aircraft flies at altitudes that will keep it within gliding distance of land and enable us to safely and efficiently serve the entire Maluku archipelago. At twice the speed of the Porter and the ability to fly 2,000 nautical miles without refueling, the PC-12 turns Brad's and my 12-hour day into an easy 3.5-hour roundtrip flight.

Seeing God turn dreams into reality has been one of the most exciting parts of serving on the YAJASI team in Papua. I am convinced that our primary task at YAJASI is to find his path and stay on it, to stay in the current of what God is doing to reach the people of Papua and the Malukus. If we're on his path, when something is truly needed for the work, we will see him provide it. After all, he loves the people of Eastern Indonesia much more than we do.

But how far will my faith stretch with that concept?

The PC-12's price tag was $3.4 million. That's more than the combined total funding that Wycliffe and JAARS had raised for all previous aircraft in their 50-year history. We were painfully aware of this fact. Honestly, I felt uncomfortable with the number of zeros involved in fielding a PC-12 in Indonesia. I had my seasons of doubt. Were we on God's path?

And yet, as we looked at how to empower the Bible translation movement in Eastern Indonesia, we couldn't find a better option. And so, we laid it at Jesus' feet and committed ourselves to be faithful in using the equipment he'd already given us in ways that would please him.

And God provided. He used an amazing variety of people—from Sunday school children selling cookies, to wealthy businessmen writing checks—to provide the funding for a PC-12. The aircraft made an immediate, substantial impact on the ministries of numerous teams serving the hundreds of isolated language communities in the far-flung reaches of Eastern Indonesia.

Our team's dream was and is to use this tool in a way that might make the One who gave it to us break into a smile.

YAJASI's Pilatus PC-12 on approach
to a mountain runway in Papua
(Photo courtesy of Tim Harold)

13

RFA

When we ask Christ, "What next?"
we tune in and give him a chance to pour his ideas
through our enkindled imagination.
—Frank Laubach

I wiggle in my seat, sit up straight, and chant my one-line mantra: "RFA. Ready for Anything." The poor fellows who find it their unfortunate circumstance to have me checking them out in the Pilatus Porter have heard this little routine ad nauseum. Just a little ditty to get both of us on high alert as we turn onto final approach into the marginal airstrips of Papua. Tailwinds, downdrafts, pigs on the airstrip, people on the airstrip, people chasing pigs on the airstrip, pigs chasing people on the airstrip … you name it, it can happen. Flying in Papua is an RFA-intensive endeavor.

The ready-for-anything mentality extends beyond the high-risk take-off and landing window. Glenn Grubb's first training flight in the Porter to an interior airstrip illustrates the point well.

After landing at the interior government center of Mulia, Glenn and I had loaded up the aircraft with a team of medical personnel and 600 pounds of medicine. We were to take them across the mountain passes to Faowi where we would drop the team off, and I would train Glenn in operating the Porter at Faowi's airstrip.

Ready to go, Glenn's finger was on the master switch to begin the start sequence on the Porter's powerful turboprop engine. A shout from behind convinced him to hold off for a moment. Doctor John, the head of the Indonesian health department at Mulia, came running up to the aircraft. A woman in difficult labor was losing lots of blood and needed to be medevaced to Sentani. In an instant, the day's carefully laid plans for training became insignificant. Ready for Anything.

The medical team jumped out of the aircraft, and the medicines were quickly offloaded. Soon the patient was on board. She had already lost a lot of blood but was still conscious. A nurse and one of the patient's relatives climbed in as well. We prayed and got going.

We had to take a circuitous route out of the mountains, following the valleys in order to fly as low as possible for the patient's sake. I put my oxygen on her and opened the valve all the way to give her maximum flow. The nurse kept her IV flowing.

An ambulance was waiting back in Sentani. I pray that we were able to help save the lives of that Dani woman and her baby but, as is frequently the case, I never heard what happened to her.

Ready for anything. Are we? Before we were interrupted by Doctor John, Glenn and I were already doing something *good*—flying meds and medical workers to serve the Iau people in Faowi. In my own life, I frequently settle for that much: I'm doing something good, so I get on with it and unplug from a moment-by-moment listening for my Master's call. If the Great Physician comes running up to my life, how ready am I to drop my own plans, no matter how good, decent, and Christian they are? Do I even live in a way that allows Jesus' soft voice to be heard through the perpetual noise of an *always-on, always-online* lifestyle?

As Sheri and I walk this path that the Lord has beckoned us to, we are frequently challenged to ask ourselves how ready we are for the next thing on God's agenda for us. We seek to have a more prayerful RFA approach to Jesus moving in our lives. And as we move towards that path, in fits and starts, we're experiencing even richer depths of joy.

14

BOXES

If you talk to a man in a language he understands, that goes to his head.
If you talk to him in his language, that goes to his heart.
—NELSON MANDELA

I've known Zeth for a long time. Ten years. An easygoing guy, we've frequently shared light moments. Seen a lot of laughter on Zeth's face. Never seen him cry. That changed a few weeks ago.

The day started at 5:30 in the morning as a lot of my flying days do. The preflight inspection on the Pilatus Porter went fine, but we weren't able to contact our destination on the HF radio for a weather report. Four of us huddled for prayer in our dusty cargo warehouse. Zeth Nabyal, Dick Kroneman, Paul Westlund, and I asked the Lord to give us good weather in Langda.

Without a weather report, we launched in faith for Langda just after 6:00 a.m. An hour later, crossing the spine of Papua's high ranges at 13,000 feet, we held our breath, waiting for the valley beyond to come into view. As we cleared the last of the rocky peaks, we were rewarded with the exhilarating sight of the Langda valley opening before us without a cloud in sight. Thank you, Lord.

Soon the Porter's turbine engine was spooling down on Langda's aircraft-carrier-like runway. At 6,100 feet above sea level, this 1,300-foot-long shelf of land juts out from the otherwise near-vertical terrain around it, almost like God put it there thousands of years ago to serve one day as an airstrip. As I swung out of my seat, I could see that Zeth was already out of the airplane, untying the cargo net that secured a stack of plain brown boxes in the cabin behind his seat.

I began helping, releasing the buckles on the cargo straps. "Zeth, wasn't that extraordinary how God answered our prayers and kept the weather open for us to make it in here today?"

Zeth tried to respond, but the words stuck in his throat. Zeth's hands were still working on untying some ropes. I watched them begin to tremble as he lost the struggle to control his emotions. Working through the tears that now flowed freely down his face, Zeth began to unload the Word of God in his own mother tongue. I looked over at Dick. He was just standing there quiet, alone in his thoughts. The boxes in Zeth's hands represented a 20-year labor of love for Dick, Margreet, and a team of committed Una men and women. They had given their life's work for this moment.

Zeth Nabyal chokes up unloading precious cargo in Langda—
the Scriptures in his own Una language.

Born in a simple hut with a grass roof, Zeth joined the first generation of Una to emerge from the Stone Age. Around the time of his birth, the light of the gospel reached into the Langda valley and brought freedom from oppressive spiritual powers that bound the Una people in endless cycles of killing and witchcraft. That freedom led to opportunities never before seen for the Una. Given a chance to get an education on the coast, Zeth made the most of his opportunities and pursued schooling in electronics. Eventually, he ended up becoming part of the YAJASI team, working in our avionics department. From a grass hut to aircraft electronics—a pretty amazing journey.

From the airplane, the people formed a festive procession to the church, the boxes reverently cradled on bow-and-arrow racks. Zeth was by no means alone in being unable to keep his joy from overflowing into tears. Unbridled rejoicing and dancing—complete with the awe-inspiring Una war cries—were followed by a time of quiet reverence as we were led in prayer by an Una pastor. I cannot remember when I've been so moved.

A few days later I was again landing in Langda. This time the airplane was full of guests coming to attend the formal celebration and dedication of the Una New Testament.

The Una people staged an elaborate drama depicting the cycle of violence and fear that once held them firmly in its grip. They celebrated the freedom that the gospel of Jesus Christ brought them, and now the wonder of having his words speak to them from these pages in their own language. For many of them, it was far beyond what they could ask or imagine.

At one point during the festivities, the organizers had thirty or so key members of the translation team line up on the uneven hillside. As the clouds swirled around us and misty droplets clung to our clothes, each member was given a copy of the Una New Testament. When the church leader distributing the Bibles got to Zeth, they were both beaming wide smiles. Then their eyes met. I saw a deep connection between these two Una men, a profound understanding as to what this book really meant. The smiles melted away, and they locked each other in an embrace and wept with abandon.

The boxes of Bibles were ceremoniously
carried on Una men's bows.

The joyous procession from the airstrip up to the church in Langda

The embrace

I was trying to photograph the moment, but it will live only in my memory—I had to turn and walk away.

Moments later, my composure regained, I returned to see Zeth and the others clutching these books to their chests as though someone had just given them a gift they hadn't ever dared hope for.[11] Then, in unison, they raised the *evidence* that God speaks Una high in the air. Zeth's face said it all: triumph, defiance, relief... YES!

As long as I live, I will never forget this moment.

I glimpsed heaven in the Langda valley that day, and I will remember those moments for as long as I live. I have an unpayable debt to those who sent us there, to the very end of the earth, to be a part of this.

We have given nothing and gained everything.

---

11 I snapped a photograph of this moment (opposite page), which now hangs in the William Cameron Townsend Building at the JAARS Center in Waxhaw, North Carolina.

Zeth Nabyal clutches treasure to his chest.

15

FIRE MAN

Then God said, "Let us make mankind in our image, in our likeness."
—THE BOOK OF GENESIS

I'm not a very good fire starter. Sometimes it takes me half an hour to get a fire going. That's if I'm using newspaper, kerosene, and a lighter. Go camping with me sometime and you'll see what I mean. Must be bad kerosene.

Occasionally I hang with folks who really aggravate my complex about my fire-starting abilities.

As I approached the mountains 100 miles south of home, the early morning skies were crowded with heavy, wet clouds. Large areas of the view out of the airplane's windshield were gray with rain. Still, when I radioed my destination, the village of Omban, they reported that the weather in their tiny little pocket of a valley was open. And so, I pressed on, weaving my way between the heavier rain cells through narrow corridors where the visibility was better. I called Omban several more times on the radio, and each time received the same assurance that the weather there was still open.

And it was, if only just. The mountain walls had clouds on all of them right down to the treetops, and rain was moving in from the higher ranges to the south. The angled approach path was clear of cloud and rain.

We made it in without much difficulty. We hadn't been on the ground long when the rain started, and the weather in the valley closed in completely. Based on the larger weather pattern I'd seen on my way in, I knew I wasn't going anywhere anytime soon. I had some passengers with me that were continuing on the flight. They were stuck too.

My friend Andi, the local pastor, was there at the airplane. Probably 50 years old, Andi is a passionate follower of Jesus. My passengers, Andi, and I stood under the Pilatus Porter's wing in a futile effort to stay dry. In my mind's eye, I picture a Swiss aeronautical engineer nursing a hot cup of coffee and a deep grudge against bush pilots. He smiles as he tweaks the design of the wing so that no matter where the luckless pilot stands, rain water will drip with diabolical precision between the nape of his neck and the open collar of his shirt, daring him not to say a bad word. I know this particular conspiracy theory is true because you can stand under the wing of a Helio Courier all day while the heavens pour forth without getting so much as a drop on you … or even *thinking* a bad word. I set aside thoughts of laying my hands on my imaginary engineer, and instead I asked Andi if we could hang out in one of the *honais*—the Ketengban tribe's grass-roofed huts—that line the airstrip at Omban. We would be drier in a structure built with stone-age tech than we would be under the precision-built 20th-century aluminum wing of an airplane. We ran through the rain to the nearest bachelor's hut and joined a dozen or so young men already ensconced around the warmth of the clay fire pit in the center of the floor.

The Ketengban are generous to a fault, and I soon had a steaming hot sweet potato in my hands, plucked out of the coals. When I finished my breakfast, I leaned back against the axe-hewn planks that formed the walls of the honai and just enjoyed the company.

Our conversation meandered for a while. I noticed a subgroup of the young men, holding their own conversation across the fire from me. Andi was listening in. Since they were speaking their native Ketengban language, I couldn't understand them.

"What are they talking about, Andi?" I asked in Indonesian, which he spoke as well.

"They're just carrying on about how amazing it is that they have an honest-to-goodness pilot in their hut," says Andi.

Here we go again with the hero worship bit.

"Listen up, guys," I said. "How many nails did you use when you built this honai?"

They looked at the floor, and one of them sheepishly said, "None." In this little mountain village, the use of modern materials is a sign of status, wealth, and forward-thinking. To them, I was pointedly calling attention to how backward and primitive they were.

"Look around you. We've got fourteen full grown men in here, sitting on this beautiful woven rattan floor suspended 3 feet off the ground where the critters can't get to us. It's pouring rain outside; we're completely dry. The fire pit is keeping us toasty warm … and cooking breakfast for us. And you did all this *without a single nail*? I couldn't build something like this if my life depended on it. You guys have mastered your environment.

"How long can you guys survive out in the jungle?" I asked. They all gave me blank stares. They'd never heard a question like that before. How long? They started to laugh nervously because they couldn't figure out where I was going with this.

"Indefinitely, right?"

They didn't answer, but their faces said, *Yeah, duh.*

"Put me out in the jungle without one of you guys to nursemaid me, and in two weeks I'm dead." They all started laughing again. They thought I was kidding. There's no way that someone as smart as a pilot could be that incompetent.

"No, really. I'm serious. *Dead* dead. Put-me-in-the-ground-and-say-some-nice-things-about-me dead." Just above the soft sounds of the raindrops pummeling the grass roof above our heads you could hear murmurs passing through the group—the Ketengban equivalent of low whistles.

"I can't hunt to save my life. I've never shot a bow and arrow, much less made one from jungle materials. And even if I did somehow manage to catch some game, how would I cook it? I haven't a clue how to make a fire without matches. How do you guys do it?"

"Well, nowadays we try to carry matches in plastic bags with us when we're in the jungle, but we still store fire-starting stuff in special dry places throughout our territory. Mostly in caves," they replied.

"Can you show me how you do it?" I asked. One young guy jumped up and ran outside into the rain. In the *rain*. I'm thinking, *He's gonna gather materials in the pouring rain and make fire?*

Our man is back in no time with a bundle of stuff. He takes a 2-foot-long stick and, using a knife, shaves off a small pile of fine shavings. He then takes the same stick and splits one end of it. He pries apart the stick and shoves a small stone into the space; the stone holds the split in the stick apart. He grabs a bunch of leaves, moss, and grass that he had gathered out in the rain—they look mostly dry—and places them on the floor, then places the stick with the stone in it down on top of them. He then whips out a length of split rattan vine and loops it around the outside of the stick. In the space held open by the stone he places the fine shavings. Mind you, he does this all in a fluid process that takes at best a minute or two.

Ketengban fire-making tech. The stone that holds the split
in the wood open is actually wet from the rain outside.

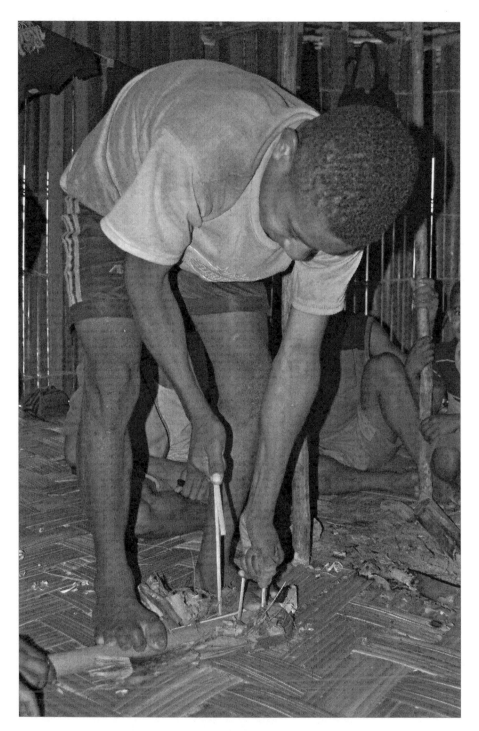

"Sawing" the rattan vine back and forth under the
assembled fire-making materials

He presses an adolescent kid into service and has him stand on the stick, holding it firmly down against the pile of tinder on the floor. The boy, bent over at the waist, holds an end of the rattan strap in each hand and begins to rapidly "saw" the rattan back and forth around the outside of the stick.

In no time—like *4 seconds*—the friction births a tiny little tendril of smoke.

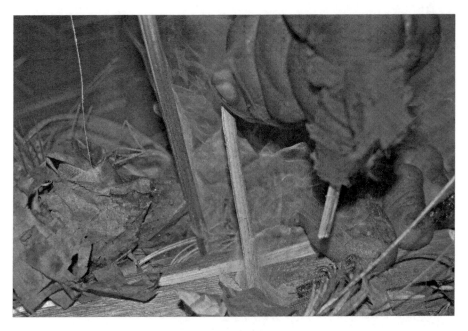

The first tendrils of smoke

The sawyer's job is done, and then the first guy takes over again. He gets down on his knees and breathes gentle caresses on that fragile wisp of smoke.

The smoke gets bigger and is soon showing signs of an attitude. Another moment passes and a tiny lick of flame spits out of the tinder, then quickly engulfs the entire pile of leaves that my new friend is holding in his hands. From starting the saw to full flame: *under 60 seconds*.

Fire Man tosses the flaming bundle into the fire pit, and I say, "Do you see what I'm talking about? You have mastered the challenges of your environment. I've mastered the challenges of my environment, which include things like computers and airplanes, but I'm no different than you.

Fire Man gently coaxes a flame to life.

The Ketengban people's remarkable mastery of their environment
enables them to create fire with just the materials at hand …
in a process that takes less than 60 seconds.

"You're made in the image of the living God, which means you carry his creativity in your souls, and you apply it to solving problems like how to build a wooden home without nails and create fire without a Zippo.

"You carry dignity because you reflect the creativity of your Creator."

16

OF OLD MEN AND LITTLE BOYS

*May God bless you with enough foolishness to believe
that you really can make a difference in the world.*
—FRANCISCAN BLESSING

He looked to me to be about 75. He came wobbling unsteadily up to the airplane. One gnarled hand firmly clasped a walking stick and the other was wrapped around his daughter's arm. I couldn't help wondering what sights this man must have seen in his lifetime: He was of the generation that went from complete isolation in this mountain valley straight into the twenty-first century.

He wasn't seeing much of anything at the moment. Opaque cataracts enveloped both of his eyes. As he didn't speak any Indonesian, I asked bystanders to ask him if he'd ever been on an airplane before. He hadn't. Can you imagine stepping out of the Stone Age, into an aircraft for the first time … *with no sight*? Through the interpreters, I told him that it would be very noisy and at times the airplane might wobble around like a canoe in rapids. He let out a low whistle and grasped hold of my arms tightly, as if to say, "Take good care of me, young man."

Back at home base, as we gently lifted the old man onto an empty cargo cart, we took a moment to ask the Good Doctor to guide the human hands of the doctors who would perform his cataract surgery.

***

"How old is your son?"

I needed to know whether he was older than 2 years to determine, as per regulations, whether he needed his own seat or could be held on his dad's lap.

"He's 5," the father answered. "He's been sick for a long time," he added, by way of explanation. "We need to go to the hospital." The Mek people of Nipsan are of very short build, but it was very hard for me to believe this tiny guy was already 5 years old. His stomach was grotesquely distended … but his smile was brilliant. I dropped to my knees in the dirt, embraced this precious child, reminded him that he was made in the image of the Creator of the universe and lifted him up in prayer.

***

The last Friday of every month, we stop flight operations and commit the morning to a time of worship, hearing from the Word and prayer. We're pretty strict about refusing all flight requests for this one day a month. Our speaker one Friday, a passionate Indonesian missionary, had finished his talk and slipped out for another commitment. His words had been moving. Simple yet powerful. I wanted to thank him, so I ran after him and out the front door of the hangar. There, instead of finding my friend, I was confronted with an old man, literally waiting on the doorstep of our locked-down facility. He'd just gotten news that his son, in his home village in the interior, had been bitten by a snake and died. "Please!" he wept, "Please fly me back to my village!"

I thought of our commitment to take a rest from our busy flight operations—for about a half second. A quick check assured that we had the resources to make the flight in the afternoon. The airplane met a man in the midst of his pain and became a conduit of compassion.

***

Flying airplanes, no matter how exotic the locale and challenging the environment, eventually becomes routine. The treasure that many of us at YAJASI have found lies off the path of aviation. The real treasure is in the moments where we have the opportunity to touch the lives of some of the most marginalized, forgotten people on the planet. To recognize in them the dignity, worth, and value that being created in the image of God has given them. These moments are treasure that no wealth can gain and no poverty can take.

17

A Tale of Two Villages

[There is] the idea that if you leave things alone you leave them as they are. But you do not. If you leave a thing alone you leave it to a torrent of change.
—G.K. CHESTERTON

A lone string of clouds clung to the ridge on final approach. I angled the Porter slightly to the left and felt my senses sharpen as the grim sight of aircraft wreckage blurred past the left side of my peripheral vision.

Passing the committal point, we rejoined the normal approach path and within seconds were flaring over the lip of the cliff that marks the beginning of Omban's steeply sloped airstrip. We were soon parked at the top of the airstrip and my passengers, guests from the United States, stepped out of the airplane and into another world. The hamlet on the west side of the airstrip was a cluster of round huts. Smoke from morning cooking fires lazily drifted through the thatched roofs.

Soon Pilipus, a wizened old guy who remembers the bygone days well, was telling us what life was like before the gospel entered this valley. He himself had killed five people … and eaten them. When I asked him what would happen to him when he died, he confidently responded, "Ah, my body is just an object; they'll put it in the ground. But me? I'll go up to my new house in heaven!" I told him that we would be sure to drop in on him there.

Pilipus. Formerly a killer, now a man of peace
(Photo courtesy of Clive Gray)

A Yali man looks down the airstrip at Kosarek after we'd landed.
(Photo courtesy of Clive Gray)

We wandered through the hamlet, greeting people, holding babies,[12] taking up invitations to step inside a few of the huts. Our guests were given precious gifts: a grass skirt, a net bag, a headdress of bird of paradise feathers, and a cassowary thigh-bone dagger. We soaked up the warmth of these dear people. We could have stayed here all day, but there was another hamlet on our agenda.

A breathtaking 30-minute flight puts us over the village of Kosarek. Final approach is over a deep gorge to a short airstrip perched on a shelf 4,500 feet above sea level. Again, my senses are on high alert. Kosarek is one of a few places in Papua where I've genuinely scared myself.

My friend Ananias' warm smile greets our group. Most others hang back. There's a different spirit here, and to my guests, the aura is palpable. What is it? While there are a few precious believers here—and Ananias is one such bright spot—this people group's acceptance of the gospel has been nowhere near as complete as Omban's. There is still the presence of the old darkness and fear that has long permeated these valleys.

So why the difference between the two villages? At least part of the explanation lies in the fact that in 1998 the people of Omban received the New Testament in their own language. They have a Bible school that trains pastors and evangelists using the Scriptures in their own tongue. Their hunger for the Word of God is such that they established a carefully selected team to work on the translation of the Old Testament. The living Word of God is having a tangible impact in the lives of the people of Omban.[13]

In Kosarek, the journey towards receiving the Word has been fraught with obstacles. But there is light on the horizon. Mike and Amy Martin, partnering with a group of men from Kosarek, are working hard to give these people the opportunity to see the path to freedom in words that speak to their hearts.

And what a thing to throw your life away for: to see the Kosarek people, and scores of other people groups like them, experience the fullness of joy and freedom that God has for them.

---

12 It was on this visit to Omban that the events of chapter 26, "Dry Baby," took place.

13 The Shorter Old Testament in Ketengban was completed in 2014. See chapter 60, "Cheaters."

18

Church in a Very Small Place

Foxes have dens and birds have nests,
but the Son of Man has no place to lay his head.
—Jesus of Nazareth

Papua is one of the few areas of Indonesia that is considered Christian. The local church I attend built a large new structure for the express purpose of being able to do ministry better. I don't see how the cavernous structure has changed us much. I don't see a lot of evidence that it helps us do ministry any better either.

About the time our church building was finished, I had to make a quick trip to the opposite end of the archipelago. While there, I stayed in the home of an Indonesian friend and colleague. This part of the country is definitely not considered Christian, nor is it particularly friendly to those who call themselves by that name. The evening I arrived, my friend had a "church meeting" to attend. I asked if I could go along. He discouraged me from going but eventually relented, and we left his home as evening fell.

I have no idea where we ended up because we drove for over an hour through dark, winding back streets until we stopped in front of a small unfinished house in a long row of small unfinished houses. My friend and I went inside, joining a group of about fifteen other men. The windowless room had no furniture whatsoever. Completely bare.

We sat along the walls on the concrete floor. The meeting started with a time of worship. It was unbelievable. A guy gently strummed a guitar, and the rest of us sang softly—we couldn't let anyone outside hear what was going on. Halfway through the second song a torrential rain started. Now we sang with abandon. No chance anyone would hear us with the clamor of the rain on the tin roof. My friend shared from the Word. Then they had a time of sharing their burdens with each other. It was only at this point that I realized that these men enjoying this sweet fellowship were a pretty eclectic bunch of Jesus followers. They covered the denominational and doctrinal spectrum: a Pentecostal, a Catholic, several evangelicals, a member of a liberal denomination, and I don't remember the labels I'm supposed to use for the rest of them. Their own fellowships had no church buildings (and very few members), so these guys met here regularly to worship.

Tonight, the agenda was to find a way to respond to a letter from militants threatening these Christians in response to their plan to build a small prayer room structure out of bamboo. I was essentially a fly on the wall and watched the peace-filled, harmonious way this diverse group processed a volatile issue. Jesus was there. Unity was there. Love, across enormous cultural and theological divides, was there.

Later a bunch of us crammed into my friend's car to head home. I sat in the back and listened to these men yearn for the day when they could have a *real* church building. I told them I attended a church with a beautiful, spacious building—we even have benches to sit on!—but I would give anything for my church body to experience what they had shared together in that cramped, stuffy, unfurnished room. I think they thought I was nuts when I told them I suspected that if they ever got their wish, they would miss these clandestine nights of sweet fellowship.

19

A MISSING AIRCRAFT

Concentration on God is strenuous,
but everything else has ceased to be so.
… If he is there, the universe is with me.
—FRANK LAUBACH

I was weary. Weary from six hours of futile searching for a missing aircraft. Weary from the thought of having to go out and do it all over again the next day. And maybe the next, and the day after that… Weary from the thought of all the important ministry flights we were cancelling to help the local operator find their lost and presumed-crashed airplane. Weary from the hours of heightened concentration and alertness needed to safely conduct search and rescue operations in mountainous terrain. As I peeled myself out of the aircraft's seat, I told a teammate that I really didn't want to go back out the next day.

But, at 4:30 the next morning I found myself preparing for another day of searching. We gathered in the dark, waiting for enough light to launch towards the search area. Four YAJASI crew and three men from Search and Rescue (SAR) bowed our heads to pray. I knew that the SAR guys didn't share my faith, but I also knew we had only one source of help to look to. I prayed in the name of Jesus, declaring before all present that "only you, Jesus, can lead us to this missing aircraft." The gauntlet was down. His honor was on the line.

We launched as the first signs of the new day were stirring on the Pacific Ocean to our east. An hour later, as we approached the area we planned to search, our path was blocked by cloud and rain. Forced to abandon my carefully thought-out search plan, we were pushed in a different direction as we navigated along the edge of the storm.

About halfway along the perimeter of the bad weather, there was an opening through the clouds that led directly towards the area I had planned to search first. Excited, I began to bank the aircraft towards the break in the clouds.

Go straight.

Paul Westlund, in the seat next to me, hadn't spoken. The voice was quiet and calm. I recognized it. I stopped the turn and headed back around the outer edge of the storm. Paul gave me a quizzical look but didn't say anything. I didn't say anything either. I'm not sure "I heard a voice in my head" would have cut it.

Ten minutes later, we were finally able to turn the corner on the weather and once again head towards the mountains. But here, the picture was different, and different in a discouraging kind of way. On the other side of the storm, only one peak was visible; all the rest were covered in a wet blanket of clouds. And, as we approached the mountain, we could see clouds were also closing in on this one remaining peak. Our huge search area had been reduced to the summit of a single mountain … and it was quickly disappearing.

We wouldn't have much time, but it was worth a quick look. I slowed the aircraft down and extended 28 degrees of flaps—the optimum configuration for SAR operations close to terrain. We began our first pass.

Almost immediately:

I've got him!

I recognized the voice. It was Paul's. Quiet and calm had been replaced by a shot of adrenalin.

We were able to make one additional pass over the crash site—enough to know there would be no survivors—and then the clouds closed in. Less than 5 minutes had elapsed since we arrived over the mountain.

The clouds close in as we make a pass over the crash site (circled).

Go straight.

Unmistakably, God had circumvented my plans—plans that almost certainly would have caused us to arrive in the area too late, after the mountain top had closed over with clouds. Instead, he led us directly to the missing aircraft and brought honor to his name.

Upon returning to base, in the general press of people meeting our aircraft, I didn't get a chance to speak with the SAR guys who were on our airplane. But I hope they were wondering,

Who is this Jesus who answers prayer like this?

20

THE END IS NEVER THE END

I shall not waste my days in trying to prolong them.
—JACK LONDON

It's not often that my day starts in a VIP facility and ends in the mud of a mountain airstrip, but this is Papua and you never know what a day will hold.

Our little Pilatus stood out like a sore thumb on the tarmac of Sentani's airport. Parked in front of the VIP arrival lounge, it was dwarfed by Boeings on every side. Eventually the vice governor of Papua and his entourage made their way to our aircraft. Our mission? Deliver them to the celebration of the Kimyal people receiving the Word of God in their own language.

An hour later, with the aircraft safely parked at the top of the Koropun airstrip, the dedication ceremony is in full swing. A pastor is speaking to the assembled crowds. I wander about with my camera, watching faces, taking it all in. Under the brilliant blue sky and towering mountain walls that surround us, the Kimyal are resplendent in their best dress. I spot a guy in his warrior finery standing next to a man in the uniform of a government civil servant. In Papua, the Stone Age and the twenty-first century dance together with a tentative step and uncertain rhythm.

Dressed to celebrate, the Kimyal came to Koropun from the
farthest reaches of their territory.

Then, through a maze of bird of paradise plumes I notice it. A simple,
chest-high monument with a tiny brass plaque embedded in it. I quietly
maneuver to the point where I can read the engraving.

Philip J. Masters
April 9, 1932
Sept 25, 1968
My Faithful Martyr
Revelation 2:13

My mind floods with thoughts and images. 1968. He was 36 years old.
I was a newborn. These mountains surrounding me were then solidly in
Satan's grip. The Kimyal and their Yali neighbors were fierce defenders
of the evil one's domain. Fully aware of the risks, Masters walked in,
hoping to pierce the darkness with the light of God's passionate love for
these people. He didn't walk out. The bows of Yali warriors sent dozens

A simple plaque next to the airstrip in Koropun bears tribute to a
man who was killed by those he was attempting to reach.

of arrows into his body, and his life bled away on a lonely riverbed a few
valleys west of where I stand.[14]

The End.

It was the end of a life full of hopes and dreams. The end of Phil's time
to be a husband to his wife and a father to his children. The premature
end of his life was, and is, a tragedy. And yet…

My eyes refocus on this huge gathering of Kimyal beside the Koropun
airstrip. I've met several who have trekked days through the mountains
to get here. They walked those mountain trails in peace, in a complete
absence of fear that they would be ambushed by their enemies or, worse,
overwhelmed by evil spirits.

Today, among the Kimyal, the spirit of happiness, freedom, and light
is palpable. Phil Masters gave his life for this end. For this day.

I look again, and there's Phil's widow, forty-two years after her husband's death, lifting a ceremonial net bag to reveal a stack of freshly
printed books whose pages contain some very good news for the Kimyal.

---

14 For the full story of the martyrdom of Phil Masters and Stan Dale, read *Lords of the Earth:
An Incredible but True Story from the Stone-Age Hell of Papua's Jungle* by Don Richardson
(Bethany House Publishers, 2008).

Not far from the monument dedicated to her martyred husband,
Phyllis Masters lifts a ceremonial net bag unveiling the first copies
of the Kimyal New Testament.

The one who lost so much gives that which has sustained
her to those who stole so profoundly from her.

Holding the first copy of the Word of God in his own language,
the man who received the gift from Phyllis Masters shares
the story of his own transformation.

Phyllis Masters presents the first New Testament to a wizened warrior. The one who lost so much gives to a representative of those who stole so profoundly from her. She gives what has sustained her these many years.

> *You have heard that it was said,*
> *"Love your neighbor and hate your enemy."*
> *But I tell you, love your enemies.*

I thought I knew beauty, but nothing compares to this. This moment is *beautiful*.

I'm thinking, *Why is God so generous to me that I get to stand with unseen angels and witness this glimpse of heaven come to earth?* And then, a prayer: Lord, may those of us who follow in Phil's footsteps be found worthy of his example. May we follow you with the same unquestioning devotion.

21

THE WRONG AIRPLANE

May God bless you with the gift of tears
to shed with those who suffer from pain ...
or the loss of all that they cherish.
—FRANCISCAN BLESSING

The runway at Okpahik clings like an epaulet to the shoulder of a 10,000-foot mountain in Papua's eastern highlands. This is an airstrip with a lot of issues. So many, in fact, that after more than twenty years of flying in Papua, I still consider it as one of the most difficult.

Why? It's *high*: 6,000 feet above sea level. Because of the thin air at this altitude, the airplane's speed is 12% faster at touchdown than it is at sea level, so things are happening that much faster.

It's *short*: 1,000 feet long—that's the normal amount of runway that an airline pilot *leaves behind him* on landing.

It's *steep*: the touchdown zone has a 15% slope—right at our maximum slope limit. It's so steep it is actually difficult to walk on when wet without losing your footing. In the United States, the maximum allowable grade when constructing a road is 7%. Think of the steepest hill you've ever driven up, double the slope and you've more or less got the picture. We're literally landing on the side of a mountain.

Oh, and one other thing. It *disappears*.

Not kidding. It's convex in shape (like the surface of a sphere), with the slope of the airstrip tapering off at the top, and because the airstrip sits transverse (perpendicular) to the overall slope of the mountain it's on, when you pitch the nose of the aircraft upwards to flare for landing*, everything you have been looking at disappears, and your windshield fills with empty sky. Picture landing on an orange: you pitch the airplane up to match the 15% convex slope and suddenly you see only empty space. You're blind. It is the only place I've ever landed where this occurs. I happened to be the one to make the first landing for YAJASI at Okpahik. I have no shame in admitting that when I experienced this disappearing runway phenomenon for the first time, my insides turned to jello and my courage went walkabout.

On short final to Okpahik. Due to the runway's convex shape, the
top of the airstrip disappears from view as you touch down
(Photo courtesy of Steve Morrell)

And then there's the *weather*. On a clear day, Okpahik is a handful. But days there are seldom clear. Cruelly, the airstrip sits at a point on the mountain where the prevailing winds tend to wrap a band of constantly moving clouds across the airstrip. One hundred feet higher or lower on the mountain and the airstrip would mercifully be outside the path of this almost perpetual band of clouds. Several times I have landed with the approach path completely clear, taxied to the top of the airstrip and parked, and before the engine's one-minute cooldown period was complete, I was completely enveloped in clouds. I could see only a few yards down the airstrip on which I had just landed.

And finally, it can get *windy*—so much so that we've put a "wind curfew" on Okpahik: no landings after 9:00 a.m.

I've had plenty of landings where I'm sure my passengers, were they not polite, would have asked if I actually possessed a pilot's license. ("Son, did we land? Or did we get shot down?") Out of all the earth-airplane collisions I've been a party to (charitably called "landings"), I performed far-and-away my worst one ever at Okpahik.

The final approach was clear, but there were some clouds moving around just off the left side of the airstrip. It's not that unusual to have clouds so close to the final approach course. I made my committed call-out* on short final, just before I came abeam those clouds. As the clouds zipped past on my left, I got a huge sense of acceleration and just about lost my equilibrium—I felt like my head spun *backwards*. I was fast approaching the dirt and had an overpowering sensation of going long on the airstrip, so I chopped the power—bad idea—and pitched the airplane up for the flare. I slammed into that 15% slope harder than anything I'd ever done in my student pilot days. The airplane was fine, and the experience served as a profound aid in the continual fight with my own pride. Still, not something I'd want to repeat on a regular basis.

The key to having a more successful arrival at Okpahik is to leave our home base of Sentani as soon as the control tower opens at 6:00 a.m. You'll then arrive overhead the airstrip as early as possible in the morning, with the highest chance of clear skies and calm winds. It's not uncommon for wind and cloud to make Okpahik unworkable from 7:30 onwards.

This particular morning was going great. Arriving at the hangar at 5:15, the weather was gorgeous. Our ground operations team had the aircraft loaded in record time, and soon my preflight inspection was complete. I grabbed the maintenance release clipboard in the airplane to sign off the airplane as being airworthy and released for flight. When I did, I found to my surprise that the aircraft didn't have any flight time left on it—it needed to come into the shop for its required 100-hour inspection. We couldn't legally fly the airplane. A breakdown in communications meant that we had just about launched in the wrong airplane. The right airplane sat only 20 yards away on our ramp, but it was now 6:00 a.m., and I wanted to be wheels-up on my way to Okpahik. To make matters worse, I had a brand-new pilot with me coming on his first ride-along flight to Papua's interior. Any desire to make a good impression of how smoothly we ran our flight operations was shot to pieces. My perfect morning was ruined, and frustration burned in my spirit. Impolite thoughts burned in my brain—in two languages.

Knowing that it would take at least another full hour to switch over to the new aircraft, and that all the while our window of opportunity for getting into Okpahik would be shrinking, I considered cancelling the flight. I walked up to my office, closed the door, took a deep breath, and asked Jesus what I should do.

A few minutes later, I left my office with a sense of peace and purpose. Our long-suffering ground ops guys moved the 1,500 pounds of cargo over to the new airplane and tied it down (probably wondering all the while if being dimwitted was a prerequisite for being a pilot … or if we develop the capacity with practice). I did my second preflight inspection of the morning.

We launched almost two hours late. About 10 minutes out of Okpahik, I get a call on the HF radio. It's Yuli in the village of Okbap. He's telling me something about my friend Pies (pronounced P.S.). I can't quite make out what he's saying, so I ask him to repeat it. The second time the message is clear enough to understand: "Pies' wife passed away overnight in the village of Maksum" (which at this point in time did not have an open airstrip). If I could help, they would carry her body over the trail to the airstrip at Okbap, and would I be able to take her from there to her home village of Bime? I told them I'd be there in half an hour.

My heart was heavy for Pies. One of our family's close friends, Pies is an orphan from the village of Bime. He was raised by relatives in the village of Maksum, 40 miles east of Bime. Pies had lived out on the coast for around fifteen years working for a number of missionary families, including ours. Pies doesn't know how old he is, but I'd guess he was around 35—and most of us figured he was going to be a confirmed bachelor. But a year prior to this, Pies surprised us and returned to his home area in the mountains to find a wife. And in the village of Bime he was successful. Having been married a few short months, he decided to take his new bride to visit his adoptive parents in Maksum—a tough week-long trek through the mountains. On the last day of the journey, his young wife fell ill. He and his companions carried her into the village of Maksum. She didn't last the night.

Pies in happier times (Photo courtesy of Tammy Harold)

The weather at Okpahik was beautiful. Not a cloud in the whole valley and the wind was dead calm. Amazing. After quickly unloading our cargo, we were airborne again for the short 12-minute flight to Okbap. We landed at 9:40, 20 minutes before Okbap's 10:00 a.m. wind curfew.

Just after we shut down, a throng of people came up the hill from Maksum. Four guys carrying a homemade stretcher were in the center of the group. I didn't see Pies, but then, at all of 4 feet tall, he's easy to miss in a crowd. As the group approached the airplane, a short guy slides out of the crowd and heads towards me. For an instant I didn't recognize him—he's skin and bones—the trip was hard on him too, apparently.

We embrace. Pies' face is buried in my chest, and he's sobbing into my shirt. I wasn't ready for this, and I break down.

As the tears of heartbreak roll down our faces, like so many others before me, I ask, *Why, God? You care for the poor. You care for the orphans. Here's Pies, finally married after all these years of being alone, and after three months you let his wife die?* I stood on the top of that mountain airstrip clutching my friend, feeling his grief more than I've ever felt anyone else's … and crying like I haven't cried since I was a kid.

The two of us must have been a sight. Here's this tiny tribal guy, most of his teeth gone, carrying his possessions in a little net bag over his shoulder. And then there's me: the absurdly rich-by-comparison missionary in my clean white pilot shirt. I have seven more of these shirts at home; they wouldn't all fit into Pies' net bag. We're worlds apart, but under the wing of that airplane our souls melted together, and I felt closer to Pies than a brother.

After what feels like an eternity, I choked out a question. "What happened?"

"I don't know. She just got sick, then weak, then unconscious, and then we lost her."

"Pies, I'm so sorry."

There's just nothing else to say. After a while we finally peel apart. They have laid her body in the airplane. I climb up in the cabin to make sure everything is tied down well. One of the guys pulls back the blanket that she's wrapped in so that I can see her face. She's young. I doubt she was twenty. It dawns on me that I'd never met her.

In an animistic worldview, people don't just die. There's always a reason, and generally somebody has to pay. In this case, I knew who was going to pay, and I was determined to keep that from happening.

Pies climbed in. He probably weighed 85 pounds. Fifteen minutes later, we're landing in Bime. Her parents meet us, and we weep together. Her mom won't let go of me. They are so grateful that we've brought her back to be buried in Bime. I gather the family in close; there's probably thirty or forty people crammed under the wing of the airplane. I've rehearsed a speech on the flight from Okbap.

"Pies tells me that she knew Jesus." Heads around me nod. "So," I continue, "we know that no power of darkness could touch her. Why she had to leave us right now, I don't know. What I do know is that this is not Pies' fault. He loved his wife and did everything in his power to care for her, to keep her alive. If anyone thinks this is Pies' doing and wants to make him pay, tell me now. After I leave, I don't want to hear that you have hurt my friend."

By now, I'm not worried about the parents' reaction; they're with me. In this culture, it's the girl's uncles who are "owed" in a time of death.

The uncles nod their agreement.

***

It's not until I've leveled off on the way home that it hits me. If we'd started with the "right" airplane this morning and departed on time, we would have been almost all the way back to Sentani when the call from Okbap came through—too late to turn around and make it there before wind time.

Jesus introduced his ministry on earth by quoting from this passage in Isaiah:

> *The Lord has anointed me to preach good news to the poor.*
> *He has sent me to bind up the brokenhearted.*

And on this day, in a place so very far away in time and space from that of the prophet Isaiah, I am completely convinced that Jesus forced me off my path, using my own weakness and error—the wrong airplane—to touch the life of one of the brokenhearted he claims as his own.

22

Two Murderers

May I never boast except in the cross of our Lord Jesus Christ.
—The Apostle Paul

Let's return to X-Ray.

After years of labor, the airstrip is finally finished. We now routinely land airplanes on a reasonably flat surface, which not long ago was just another piece of jagged terrain that make up the mountains in these parts.

Final approach to Daboto is always an edge-of-your-seat affair. The short shelf of dirt rushes up at me at 75 miles an hour. Clouds on my left block the escape route. I'm committed to land. Lord, help me not to bend this thing, especially in front of all these people.

All these people? Seems like well over one hundred Moi have converged on the Daboto airstrip this morning. I don't think I've ever seen more than twenty here before.

Stepping out of the airplane, I see Rich and Karen Brown, who've now been living among the Moi for a number of years. As they walk up the airstrip towards me, their feet don't seem to be touching the ground. They are beaming.

"What's with all the people?" I ask as they reach the parking area at the top of the strip.

"God is doing an amazing thing among the Moi!" says Rich with a face-splitting grin.

After years of language learning and preparation, these Ethnos 360[15] missionaries among the Moi finally reached the point where they were able to begin their chronological teaching through the Scriptures. They started with the Creation story and were moving through the narratives to end up at the resurrection of Christ. The people had come from all the far-flung hamlets of the Moi territory, some hiking five days to get there. The initial plan was to have teaching sessions five days a week. Soon after beginning, though, the Moi insisted the storytelling be done six days a week. They refused to return to their hamlets to tend their gardens and gather food. Those from afar had consumed all the food they'd brought, and the meager resources of the village of Daboto had also been depleted. Still the people refused to return to their homes for food. The Moi were literally going hungry so they could hear the Good News.

On the day I arrived, they were finishing up the teaching of the Law. The Moi were profoundly convicted of their sins and convinced that they stood separated from their Creator. The people were urgently pushing the storytelling process forward, so they could get to the part about the promised redeemer mentioned in the stories.

"Nate, we've got all the people here, and I don't think any of them understand why you first came to them with the others in that helicopter ten years ago, and I don't think they have a clue why you keep coming back. Would you share your story with them, so they might understand what drives you?" Rich puts me on the spot.

I flash back to the year 2000. I'm standing in a small clearing in the rainforest, high on the ridge on whose flank I now stand. Not another human being in sight. An hour earlier, we'd gingerly dropped out of a helicopter onto a knife-edge ridge that a lightning strike and fire had cleared of trees. I'm waiting for my GPS to pick up a satellite fix. The rest of the team has hiked on ahead, slowly clearing a path on a compass heading that we hope will someday turn into an airstrip to reach the Moi. The hairs on the back of my neck rise as I sense that I am not alone. Unable to shake the feeling, I turn around, and find myself looking into

---

15 Formerly New Tribes Mission.

the eyes of a Moi tribesman. He has stealthily crept up behind me without me hearing the slightest snap of a twig. I am the first outsider, the first white man, Piato has ever seen.

Piato and Nate at the top of the airstrip at Daboto

Back to the present. I now stand at the top of the Daboto airstrip, in a crowd of Moi and turn to find, once again, Piato standing right behind me. I put my arm around this warrior, and my heart begins to speak.

"Some of you have murdered." Rich translates into Moi.

An image of Piato finishing off one of his wives with an axe flashes across my mind.

I continue: "I have not killed. But I have hated others in my heart, and the Redeemer has said that I am guilty of murder. I lacked only the axe."

One murderer embracing another, I continued.

"My heart was black. I was separated from my Creator—under his judgment because of my sin. But I have met the Redeemer, and he has paid my penalty for murder and washed my heart clean. This is why I have come. This is why I keep coming back. So that you also may meet this Redeemer and have him carry off your sins. That you may walk with him in the light."

115

I released Piato and picked up a tiny boy who was standing at my feet. Made in the image of the living God.

"I have come also because I have a dream that this little boy will be part of the first generation of Moi to grow up in the light, free from the constant fear and oppression of the evil spirits. The Redeemer will give you victory over the evil spirits. Please, listen to the stories and follow the Redeemer when you meet him."

The word out of Daboto these days is that many of the Moi are embracing Jesus and breaking free from bondage to evil spirits.

The Light has come.

23

UNWANTED

This is what a Christian does.
—YEREMINA OF NIPSAN

Have I said it before? I love this job.

One reason is the incredible variety of missions we fly. This morning my eight passengers were the members of two families I know really well. Larry Mathews is a former pilot from our team, now involved in a media/radio ministry in Papua. He's married to Di, who serves as our mission doctor and teaches community health. Larry and Di have three kids. Their youngest, David, by virtue of having the shortest legs in the group, sits in the far back seat of the Pilatus Porter.

Paul Westlund is another passenger, but he isn't accustomed to the role—he's the most experienced pilot on our team. He started flying in Papua when I was just barely out of high school. Since Larry hasn't been in the cockpit for a while, Paul gives him the front seat next to me so that Larry can relive his glory days. Paul sits in the back next to his wife, Lavonne, and their teenage son, Mark.

Today's mission? Fly these servants from our home base at Sentani up to Nipsan, where at 5,300 feet above sea level they will get a much-needed break in the cool of the mountains, a Christmas away from the heat of the tropics and demands of ministry.

The weather is perfect, the flight uneventful, the landing doesn't break anything important, and we're soon parked at the top of the steep airstrip at Nipsan. The beauty of the valley is breathtaking, and I'm reminded why Sheri and I have so enjoyed the breaks we've taken up here. Vertical limestone massifs tower all around us. Here and there the sheer cliffs are split as if with an axe, and from these clefts plummet some of my favorite waterfalls in all of Papua. Idyllic hamlets—groups of four or five huts—cling to slopes surrounding the airstrip, smoke from the overnight fires still drifting through their grass roofs.

Nipsan is the central village in the Mek people group. On the way into the valley, we flew by Bari, one of the newer airstrips on the edge of Mek territory. The weather at Bari was of interest to me, because for my next leg I was scheduled to fly some Mek evangelists from Nipsan down there. The entire area was blanketed with low clouds.

On the ground in Nipsan, I'm in no hurry to get moving—I want to give the sun another 45 minutes to work on lifting those clouds. The people want me to fly a load of pigs to Wamena for them to sell. I'm a bit disappointed that I can't help them today, but then Paul lets me know that he's already flown in here three times in the last couple of weeks and flown twenty-six pigs to Wamena for the people. Just like Paul to actually keep track of that kind of stuff.

My friends will be staying in the home built by the original Dutch missionaries, long since retired, who opened up this area. The cabin-like structure sits empty most of the year except for when tired coastal missionaries show up to sit by the fire for a week. With the airplane unloaded, I wander over to the house to kill some time until the weather in Bari clears up. I run into Yeremina, the mission home's caretaker. Petite in the extreme, Yeremina offsets her tininess with a huge smile and a mountain of energy. It's great to see her again. I step inside the door and notice that just off the front hallway there's a curious bundle lying on the floor. It's a gorgeous 1-month-old baby girl in a *noken*, the traditional net bags that Papuans use to hold all that is precious to them.

"Is she yours, Yeremina?"

She tells me the story. Twins were born, and, as is common in these parts, the mother planned to "throw away" the second baby. In an act that went radically against her own culture, Yeremina took the baby to raise as her own. Others thought her crazy and told her so, reminding her that she didn't have the resources to raise the child on her own.

"I know, but this is what a Christian does."

This is what a Christian does.

Christian. "Little Christ"—it's what the term means, I'm told. Four-foot-tall Yeremina, a little Christ.

"Does the baby have a name?" I ask, scooping up this soft little ball of *imago dei*.

"Neli. It means 'unwanted.'"

Nate holding a precious image-bearer
whose name means "unwanted."

Papua. Every day it seems I encounter another amazing story. I hold Neli close and am struck anew by the power the animist worldview holds—throw something this beautiful away?

After a while, Dr. Di wants a turn. Di's timing is perfect—little Neli has already done her peeing on me—and, alas, I need to get back to my day job and get these evangelists to Bari.

It takes less than 10 minutes for the Porter to climb up over the mountain wall and down into the next valley. It's a bit of work to find a hole in the clouds big enough to squeeze through, but we make it in. After spending some time with the folks in Bari, I'm soon airborne again and pointed towards home. Just one passenger joins me from Bari, so the airplane is light and climbs like a thoroughbred. I'm at altitude in no time. Gives me plenty of time to think about this tiny follower of Jesus in the isolated valley of Nipsan. Doing the right thing just because it's what little Christs do.

When I get back to our base, I find out that there are other little Christs in my midst. Paul shares an office with Brad McFarlane. Brad works as our flight scheduler and is having a rough day: He's having to turn down flight requests because we've got three airplanes down for maintenance. I stop in to encourage him with the story of Yeremina and the baby. Tears in his eyes, Brad points to an untidy box of odds and ends tucked under Paul's desk. It's precious vacation stuff: puzzles, books, favorite snacks. Brad tells me that earlier that morning, with our airplane at its maximum weight, Paul's and Larry's families offloaded some of their own things to make room for boxes of baby formula that Paul had bought for a little girl … whose name means "unwanted."

I don't know what plans God has for Neli, but one thing I'm sure of: He's going to give her a new name.

24

FLOORS

I am fond of pigs. Dogs look up to us.
Cats look down on us. Pigs treat us as equals.
—WINSTON CHURCHILL

I well remember the day in December 2004 when we pulled our first Pilatus Porter out of the 40-foot container in which it had been shipped. Talk about *new car smell*. 1.7 million dollars' worth of new car smell. Pristine, perfect, brand new, even the floor was immaculate. The last people who had cleaned it were Swiss—you could eat off this floor. The next time you're on an airline flight, when you go to the lavatory and look down at the flooring, it'll look exactly like the surface of the floor in the Pilatus Porter. I guess they use the same stuff in most airplanes, but because the Swiss haven't fussed over your airline lavatory floor, I wouldn't recommend eating off of it. For that matter, the day we took the airplane out of the container would have been the last one you'd have wanted to use that particular Pilatus Porter floor as a plate.

Our floors get messy. Just about anything and everything goes in our airplanes. If it can fit in the door, we've probably flown it at one point or another. And because we're here to serve isolated tribal people, our priorities are on meeting their needs, not keeping our planes clean.

In the highlands, the main cash crop is, um, pigs. They have an incredibly high value both culturally and economically. I just heard of a rather large specimen going for $3,000. That's a phenomenal pile of cash in these parts. I know zip about animals, but I've learned a few things about pigs over the years. I can say with a fair bit of authority born of personal experience that pigs aren't particularly clean beasts. Another thing I've learned is that if you tie them up and pile them into an airplane with a bunch of their friends, they can get excited. And the thing with pigs is, if they get too excited, their bowel control is apparently significantly impaired. So, our floors get dirty.

Don't eat off them.

I remember one of the early flights with the airplane. I had flown a pile of pigs to the main government center in the highlands to be sold at market. On arrival, one of the goodhearted fellows who was helping me unload the pigs went apoplectic upon discovering the handiwork of a pig who had gotten particularly excited. He started chewing out the villager who had accompanied his pigs on the flight.

"You can't let your pigs poop in this airplane! Can't you see it's brand new?"

I had to calm my friend down—I told him that the whole reason we acquired these airplanes was to have pigs poop in them. Really. The only access most interior Papuans have to markets is via the airplane, and it's a key part of our ministry to help them develop their communities' economies. So, the pigs get to poop on the floors.

Our aircraft floors get a lot of other not-so-pleasant stuff on them as well. We fly about one medevac a week. Some are pretty clean—people with malaria, broken bones, that kind of thing. Some get pretty messy. Gunshot wounds, folks with dysentery, women in labor. We've had at least one instance of a patient bleeding to death on a flight. He was on the losing end of a machete fight.

But no matter how messy our floors get, I wouldn't trade this job for anything else, sterile working conditions notwithstanding. One of the most rewarding parts of the ministry out here is the chance to touch some of these people that most of the world has forgotten.

People with dirty feet, climb in! I've got a clean floor for you to put them on.

25

WHAT THEY DIDN'T TEACH ME IN FLIGHT SCHOOL

If you are looking for perfect safety, you will do well to sit on a fence and watch the birds; but if you really wish to learn, you must mount a machine and become acquainted with its tricks by actual trial.

—WILBUR WRIGHT, 1901

There are only a handful of schools on the planet specifically focused on training people to serve as missionary pilots. I was fortunate enough to attend what many consider to be the best in the business. The fine folks at Moody Aviation did a standout job of teaching us aspiring bush pilots how to keep the aluminum out of the ditches, and I can say with certainty that part of the reason I'm alive today is because of the principles instilled in me in Moody's hallowed halls.

But, they didn't teach me everything I needed to know to fly successfully in the wilds of Papua. Not by a long shot. And so, in the interest of improving the quality of Moody's product, I find it my duty to offer the following list for consideration in their ongoing efforts to provide the best education for young missionary aviators. May future graduates be even better prepared than I was to answer the following critical questions:

- Does the seat belt go on the outside of the gourd, or the inside?
- If you're at an airstrip and a tribal war breaks out around the airplane, do you try to intervene, or just pick what appears to be the winning side and join them?

- If someone has ridden in a seat with a bare bottom, do you clean the cushion, or just flip it over?
- On landing, when one or both brakes fail, what is the proper prayer to recite? (I'd rather have a good piece of liturgy ready than try to wing it at such a critical moment.)
- On landing, when one or both brakes fail, if you can't remember the prayer, is it OK to close your eyes anyway?

My instructors at Moody taught me how to fly an airplane into short, unimproved mountain airstrips without excessively scaring myself. But flying in remote parts of the developing world is an experience all unto itself, and thus I consider it no small oversight that they completely neglected to teach me how to fly an airplane while:

- gagging
- crying
- laughing
- peeing
- scared
- peeing while scared
- fighting back diarrhea (a fellow pilot once lost this particular fight, which is a story that, upon threats to my well-being, will remain untold)
- panicking (if you're fighting back diarrhea, it's pretty much a given that you're panicking)
- passengers are screaming (they'll do this if they sense the pilot is fighting back diarrhea)
- pigs are screaming
- passengers are still screaming (because the pigs that were screaming got loose)

I had to learn all of the above, well, on the fly.

I suppose I shouldn't lay all of the blame at my alma mater's feet. My more experienced colleagues in Papua who showed me the ropes when I first got here are equally guilty. Here are a few things I wish someone had told me during my initial checkout in flying Helio Couriers in Papua:

- When a mom hands you her diaper-less baby to hold while she climbs in the airplane:

    - if it's a girl, hold her out at arm's length

    - if it's a boy, hold him out at arm's length and *turn him around*

    - I think Papuan babies are genetically predisposed to pee on pilots. Or maybe I just scare them.

- If you're carrying drums of fuel in the airplane, when climbing through approximatly 5,000 feet, the pressure differential between the small volume of air in the drum and the ambient air at altitude will cause the ends of the drum to bulge out with a pop. But they actually don't go *pop*, they go *WHAM!* If you don't know *WHAM!* is coming, and you have a full bladder, you are in *big* trouble. If you're living right, this happens on a day when you've already dealt with babies so you're already wet.

- Large pigs, even when hogtied and secured under a cargo net, are capable of shaking the entire airplane in flight (missionary aviators call this *pig-induced turbulence*). If you don't know this, you figure the reason the airplane is vibrating violently is because it wants to shake itself into itty-bitty pieces, and you begin using what precious mental capacity not currently devoted to panicking to review life insurance policies, wills, living trusts, and the like.

- Men of the Ketengban tribe, when frightened, will grab their neighbor's upper thigh and squeeze like an anaconda. This is simply a curious bit of Papuan trivia, unless a member of the Ketengban tribe happens to be sitting next to you in the co-pilot's seat and the thunderstorm out the window scares him—this then becomes a thing of intense personal concern. Believe me.

- When using a Sic-Sac (motion sickness bag) to pee in, always, always, always DOUBLE-BAG it. I once filled a bag almost completely full and was just exhaling a wonderful *aaaahhhh*, taking a moment to revel in my newfound relief before tossing the bag out the window. It then dawned on me that I was beginning to feel unnaturally warm. I lifted the bag from my lap up to eye level, and to my horror it was leaking out both bottom corners like an Italian fountain. By the time I got the bag out the window, it had spewed most of its contents all over the cockpit. The worst of it was explaining the mess to our maintenance team back at home base. This experience raised another question I was ill-equipped to answer: Should you trust the airplane to a mechanic who is rolling on the grass, clutching his sides, laughing like a madman?

Truth be told, the best thing my mentors at Moody gave me was a ready-for-anything attitude—this has carried the day many a time. Trying to prepare oneself for every eventuality in flying is simply exhausting. Prepare for the basics and be ready for anything that the day may throw at you.

I'm still astonished at how often I'm unprepared to handle the emotional and interpersonal challenges a day can bring. I so frequently launch into my day without being ready-for-anything in my spirit, and as such I respond to life's challenges in my flesh and, unsurprisingly, pretty much make a mess of things. On the days I succeed in preparing myself with the mind of Jesus, and I stay connected to him through the day, well, the results are remarkably different.

And I don't forget to double-bag the Sic-Sacs.

Originally published in *Air and Space Magazine* (July 2012)

26

DRY BABY

Let my heart be broken by the things that break the heart of God.
—BOB PIERCE

That last chapter was a bit hard on babies as a demographic. I feel like I need to balance things out, especially because the day before I wrote that piece, I had the privilege to hold a gorgeous baby girl in the village of Omban. She came to me dry, and she went back to Momma dry. She didn't get the memo.

There were a lot of babies at the airstrip at Omban that day. In fact, we'd had three babies on their mothers' laps on the short hop from Okbap to Omban, all of them dutifully screaming at the top of their lungs. *They* got the memo. Every missionary flight school needs a screaming baby simulator. You may be able to land an airplane on a dime, but can you do your pre-takeoff checklist while a trio of distressed babies do violence to your auditory system?

Out of all the babies at Omban, I specifically sought one out in particular, because she's special.

Two years prior, I had held *another* beautiful baby girl in Omban.[16] I can't remember if my shirt was wet after that one, but chances are good that I took a damp souvenir back to town with me that day. A few weeks

_____

16 Coincidentally, the day I held this baby girl was the day the events of chapter 17, "A Tale of Two Villages," took place.

later, I ran into that precious one's dad again, in town—he'd caught a flight out. I asked how his beautiful daughter was doing.

"She died," he replied, his voice a confluence of grief and resignation.

I was stunned. She had been a healthy little girl just a few weeks prior. Infant mortality here is such that in some places they don't name their kids until they're 4 years old. I guess thinking about *the baby* dying rather than *little Jenny* cuts down on the heartache.

So yesterday, as I got out of the airplane at Omban, I see momma holding this new gift. And there's dad, beaming with pride as he helps unload the airplane.

"God blessed you with another child!" I exclaimed.

"Yes," says the dad, "and the Lord is so good to us. We missed our first one so much. We prayed, and God gave us this baby that looks exactly like her."

I wonder if it was King David's similar experience that inspired him to write:

> *Weeping may stay for the night,*
> *but rejoicing comes in the morning.*

27

MY GREATEST NEED

Although my memory's fading, I remember two things very clearly:
I am a great sinner and Christ is a great Savior.
—JOHN NEWTON

I love reading through the treasure of Luke's Gospel. In particular, I'm fond of the familiar story of the paralyzed guy with incredible friends. Those friends disassemble the roof and lower the paralytic down to be healed by Jesus.

The interesting thing is that Jesus *doesn't* heal him. At least, not immediately.

On seeing this motley crew's faith, the first thing Jesus says is,

Friend, your sins are forgiven.

This man's deepest need wasn't to be healed, but to be forgiven. I need to sit back and think about this for a minute. The man is obviously physically messed up. He is clearly desperate for relief and healing. But Jesus looks past the obvious and sees a man who is paralyzed by sin, his soul limp and atrophied from being held in those powerful bonds for far too long. And so, Jesus heals his soul, right there on the spot.

Of course, when we keep reading, we see that Jesus did subsequently heal his physical body. We can probably safely assume that this man enjoyed a non-paralyzed body for the remainder of his 70 or 80 years on this earth, until his body broke again, permanently. Had physical healing been all this man received from Jesus, he would have been cheated by the One who was capable of giving him what he needed most.

I need to more regularly meditate on the incredible truth that I have been forgiven. My greatest need has been absolutely taken care of. Everything else is gravy. So, what were those problems I'll be facing today that kept me up half the night? At the end of my 70 or 80, they won't matter, but the fact that my sins have been forgiven will be everything.

The more time I spend chewing on the eternal implications of being forgiven, the more of an impact it makes on my life in the here and now. For years, I viewed this forgiveness like an artifact from my distant past, a theological fait accompli. But when I put myself in Luke's story, in the place of the paralytic, and imagine Jesus saying those life-giving words to me, I become overwhelmed by his love for me. And this profoundly impacts how I relate to the next thing that happens to me.

A few weeks ago, I got harassed by a drunk guy (not a terribly uncommon occurrence where I live). In the course of his tirade, he found it to his liking to haul off and hit me. Not exactly what I had planned for my evening, but as I thought about this guy, I just couldn't stop seeing myself in him. And that enabled me, for perhaps the first time in my life, to literally turn the other cheek. Perhaps I'm broken in different ways than he is, but I'm still broken, and I would be paralyzed by sin if it weren't for Jesus saying to me,

Friend, your sins are forgiven.

I am forgiven. Everything else I have pales in value.
I am forgiven. My deepest need has been met. Life is safe.

My sin, oh, the bliss of this glorious thought!
My sin, not in part but the whole,
Is nailed to the cross,
And I bear it no more.

28

A Perfect Day

If there must be trouble, let it be in my day.
—Thomas Paine

I broke ground from home base at Sentani 5 minutes after the airport opened. Landing at the Lik village of Eipomek an hour later, the sun had yet to penetrate the tight little valley, and the airstrip was still in the shadows. After landing and shutting down, I met my friend Andrew Sims at the top of the airstrip. Andrew and his wife, Anne, have worked among the Ketengban people for over twenty-five years. The plan for the day is to fly Andrew, who was on his own this trip, over to the village of Okbap, with a stop in Omban along the way—both airstrips in the Ketengban territory.

In the future I need to pay more attention to my cargo manifests. Beyond the four passengers I had from Sentani, I didn't actually know what I had on board the airplane until we were offloading in Eipomek. Turns out I had some very precious cargo indeed. About a dozen unlabeled boxes held the first Old Testament portions translated into the Ketengban language: 1 and 2 Kings. Royalty on board. What a way to start the day.

We loaded back up and headed over to Omban. Heading east, we're straight into the brilliance of the early morning sun. The cloud deck below us is a blaze of glory. Don't think I'll ever tire of the view from this office. Fifteen minutes later, we're flying the amazing approach in the Omban valley.

We're here to drop off some of those boxes—the freshly printed Scriptures will be distributed to the churches in the area. Andrew also wants to check on his house—he hasn't been "home" for a while and will be returning to Omban with Anne in a couple of weeks.

I had also brought a patient with me from Sentani to return to his home in Omban. Andrew overheard the men talking (he's fluent in Ketengban). He caught enough of the conversation to have his Spirit-led alarms start ringing. Apparently, a doctor out in town told our patient, a young man in his 20s, that he couldn't help him and that the illness he had was caused by someone putting a curse on him. The doctor's medical counsel: return to your village and figure out who put the curse on you ... and fix it. Animism, pure and simple, but from a doctor? Go figure.

Andrew asks if we can take some extra time to address the issue. I need no convincing, but he tells me how critical a moment this is in terms of the temptation for folks to slip back into the animistic beliefs that have held sway in these parts for millennia.

"If they go through with this, someone gets killed," Andrew tells me.

We find the young man sitting beside the airstrip surrounded by people listening to his story. His name is Anius, and we ask him to come over to the airplane. A number of the elders from the church join us.

Andrew asks him, "Have you given yourself to Jesus?"

"Yes."

"Completely?"

"Yes."

"Will you completely forsake going to the spirits and trust only in God to heal you?"

"Yes."

Andrew shares some more with Anius about his only hope being in Jesus. We place our arms around him. "Man, he's hot," Andrew says to me in English. I feel it too. He's racked with fever. For the next 15 minutes, six or seven ask Jesus for victory over evil and for healing of Anius' body. Andi, the pastor of the church in Omban, is the last to pray.

Andrew and I climb back in the plane and fly over the mountains to Okbap. Andrew is looking down at the raging torrents and near-vertical mountain walls and shaking his head. He tells me (again) how much he appreciates the airplane—he's made the trek between these two villages before on foot. I ask him how long it took him.

"Four days, and I was a much younger man then."

We touched down on Okbap's steeply sloping airstrip *12 minutes* after departing Omban. My math skills aren't anything to write home about, but I figure that's 3 minutes of flight time for each full day of walking.

Andrew will stay in Okbap for a couple of weeks, working with a team of Ketengban men who are drafting the Old Testament translation. I climb back into the cockpit and head north for home. On the way, I'm pondering the significance of what just happened back there in Omban. I had just read Luke chapter 9 that morning. When Jesus first sent out his disciples, their marching orders were to:

proclaim the kingdom of God and to heal the sick.

Andrew, a modern-day disciple of Jesus, striving to follow these ancient instructions of his Master, under the wing of an airplane at the top of the airstrip in Omban.

***

A week later, hundreds of miles west of Omban, I was making my *five-minute-out* call for landing at an airstrip called Lumo, when I heard Andi, the pastor at Omban, on the radio. I quickly jumped in and asked him how Anius was doing. His immediate and passionate response was, "You're not going to believe this, but from the moment we all prayed for him at the airplane, he's been well!"

29

YOU CAN HURT YOURSELF HERE

Belief is a wise wager.
—BLAISE PASCAL

Once in a while I get tasked with landing at a brand-new airstrip and checking it out for our team. Such was the case for Hitadipa, which actually had been in service since the 1960s, but none of our pilots had been there before.

Another mission aviation service operates in and out of Hitadipa regularly, so I picked the brain of their chief pilot and anyone else who would talk to me about the place. I also got my hands on the runway chart—a document that shows how the runway lays in relation to terrain, details a bunch of numbers like elevation, width, length, slope, etc., gives a textual description of how to fly the approach, and has notes on hazards unique to the airstrip.

Perusing the chart for this place was a bit like reading the warning label on a chain saw. The message that came through loud and clear was: *you can hurt yourself here.*

- Blind approach
- Early committal point
- Dogleg for takeoff

- Slippery when wet
- Bad downdrafts
- 9:00 a.m. wind curfew

Translation: you fly a long portion of the final approach without being able to see what you're landing on, the airstrip itself is crooked, and the place is closed for operations after 9:00 because the mountain winds create turbulent conditions that can fire up one's adrenal system something fierce.

I arrived overhead early in the morning when the air was still smooth and the overnight fog was just burning off. I took my time getting a good feel for the lay of the land. But eventually I had to dive in and try this thing. I managed to fly the approach and land with my heart rate below 120. As advertised, the grass surface was as slick as the snot of the dozen runny-nosed kids that ran out to the airplane after I'd corralled it to a stop.

Accompanied by some of the old guys from the village and the tag-along army of runny-nosed kids, I walked the length of the airstrip measuring things and trying to determine how well the airstrip matched the description on the chart. I used a checklist to make sure I didn't miss anything.

Walking back from the far end, I asked the oldest guy a question that wasn't on the checklist: "Anyone ever crash here?"

"Yup," he said without hesitation. "See those trees off the end of the airstrip? Years ago, a fellow took off late morning when it was really windy. He hit a downdraft and became one with those trees. All survived, but they were hurt really bad." The trees probably didn't fair very well either.

So, all the fire and brimstone on the runway chart isn't just hot air, I thought to myself.

"Wow," I said to the old guy.

"Yeah, we hauled the wreckage right over here beside the airstrip." He pointed at a nondescript area of head-high grass that we had walked past twice without it ever catching my eye.

He was soon leading me through the thick undergrowth to show me what was left of the airplane. Just pieces.

I had been following with interest a buzz on the evangelical blogosphere on the whole concept of hell. Apparently, some of us are a bit fed up with the bad image that hell is giving God and are trying to make it go away. Personally, I'm not a very big fan of hell myself. I'm not exactly sanguine about the fact that our rebellion against God will send us there either. But since I didn't make the cosmos, I find it prudent to defer to the One who did. As anti-hell as I may feel in my spirit, I'm not quite ready to write it out of my worldview.

And to those agreeable to dispensing with hell, I would gently suggest, if hell does exist, the most despicable, unloving thing God could do would be to keep it a secret. But this he does not do. There it is, in plain sight, scrawled all over the pages of Scripture, tumbling out of the mouth of Jesus and the prophets before him. Like the fire and brimstone warnings on my runway chart that tell me, *You can really hurt yourself here.* The pilots who have gone before me, and know that a downdraft at this airstrip can turn your expensive airplane into little pieces of aluminum in the undergrowth, have done a wonderfully *loving* thing by warning me about it. Doesn't make for especially pleasant reading. I could always use some whiteout on my chart and make it a lot more palatable. That's ridiculous. But to use whiteout and then hand the chart off to another pilot? That's *criminal.* Their blood would be on my hands.

As a pilot, I'm scared of downdrafts. As a soul, I'm scared of hell. And I'm grateful for the lovingly fearful descriptions of it that I read in the Bible. And I'll thank you to keep the whiteout in the drawer.

30

COMMITTED

Never yield to the apparently overwhelming might of the enemy.
—WINSTON CHURCHILL

The day after checking out the airstrip at Hitadipa, I was back. In the airplane with me was the main reason for getting checked out at the runway in the first place. What a privilege to serve long-term missionary Lois Belsey: we picked her up in the lowland airstrip of Faowi, where she had been serving the Iau people, and flew her back to her home base at Hitadipa, among the Moni people.

Typically, when landing at mountain airstrips out here, you commit to the landing at some point along the approach. This is to say that you've passed an airborne *point of no return* beyond which the aircraft is no longer capable of out-climbing or out-turning the terrain that you have lowered yourself into. You will now contact terra firma no matter what you do: you can't go around and you're committed to the landing regardless of what happens.

Hitadipa has a committal point really early in the approach—it occurs 60 seconds before touchdown and a full 30 seconds *before you're able to see the airstrip* on which you're landing. And even though there are a couple of other airstrips where this is true, it feels a bit nuts to be lowering yourself into this tight river valley with no airstrip in sight—

it's in a spur valley off to the left at the far end of the canyon—you just have to take it by faith that it's there. Soon, with nothing but rugged terrain in front of you and nothing landable in sight, you're committed to land. There's no turning back.

Committed.

Makes me think about our commitment in following Jesus in the ministries he calls us to. Some of my forebears in missions used to pack their belongings in coffins as they headed to the mission field—they knew they weren't coming back. They stepped onto ships and passed their committal points. Now? We try things out ahead of time, make sure a ministry is a good fit for us, wouldn't think of leaving our home shores without a good retirement plan, health insurance, life insurance, and, above all, an exit plan: many missionaries actually get counseled to have a fallback plan in our home country in case this whole missionary thing doesn't work out.

For the better part of a year, I camped out in the Gospel of Luke. In chapter 9, Jesus says to us,

> *Whoever wants to be my disciple must deny themselves*
> *and take up their cross and follow me.*

You may not be able to see where you're going to land yet, but if you've decided to follow Jesus, don't turn back.

31

NOT ALL HERE

My kingdom is not of this world.
—JESUS OF NAZARETH

For years, we've gone to church with a woman who is often referred to, in less-than-politically correct terms, as *The Crazy Lady*. She's not all there.

Her name is Yemima. She's probably around 50, dresses in rumpled 1970s-era dresses with lots of not-always-clean lace and frills. She wears lots of lipstick, some of it on her lips, the rest in the general vicinity. Last week the dress was an unwashed dirty-white, and the lipstick was metallic gold.

Our church services always have a time when anyone can share a story about how God is working in their lives, or simply sing a song. Frequently, different groups in the church will have practiced a musical number and come up front to share it with the rest of us. Yemima always joins these groups, even though she isn't a member, nor has she practiced with them. When the youth go up front, she's right there with them. Men's groups? You bet. She adds her soprano to the basses and tenors. Sometimes she goes up by herself, grabs the mike, and sings a shrill, wavering acapella hymn.

She's not all there.

She's someplace else.

This gets me thinking about how many times we're exhorted by the Scriptures to have our minds someplace else. My mind tends to stay firmly rooted in the here and now, on the physical realities that surround me and fill my vision.

The Apostle Paul set out God's agenda for our minds when he wrote in 2 Corinthians 4:18:

> *So we fix our eyes not on what is seen,*
> *but on what is unseen,*
> *since what is seen is temporary,*
> *but what is unseen is eternal.*

In a manner of speaking, we're urged to be *not all here*. We're to fix our vision and our minds on something that is unseen. And it occurs to me that this is how one enters the unseen realm that Jesus called the kingdom of heaven. He told us it was near—as in all-around-us near—but if we're *all here*, we can't see it. And it's only when we are *there*, in the kingdom of heaven, and not *all here* in the kingdom of this world, that many of the incredible teachings of Jesus begin to make sense.

I've got a pretty strong feeling that Yemima sees the kingdom of heaven. I think that's why she always wants to sing about Jesus. She's not all here. A bunch of her is there. I hope to grow to be like her one day.

32

Prayer of a Warrior

Christianity changes people's hearts.
It brings a spiritual transformation.
The rebirth is real. The change is good.
—Matthew Parris, British journalist and atheist

After the long, early-morning flight from Sentani, I climb out of the Pilatus Porter at the top of the Daboto airstrip. I am delighted to find Piato there waiting.

I'd brought two missionaries in, and the plan is to fly one of their colleagues in Daboto out to the closest town. There's also a pile of fragrant wood called *kayu masohi*, which the Moi people harvest from the forest as a cash crop. I'll take those sweet-smelling bundles out to market on the coast to help generate some income for the community.

But soon the missionaries are telling me of a woman, one of the Moi chief's three wives, who is very ill, and hasn't been responding to medication. This morning she's taken a significant turn for the worse. Under the wing of the airplane, the Moi people conduct a long, drawn-out community discussion and eventually decide they want to send her out to receive medical care. The chief and one of his sons will go along.

Over the years, I've seen Papuan ingenuity produce a variety of innovative stretcher designs, using nothing but jungle materials, but this one was a first for me: they carried this poor woman up to the airplane in a *noken*. Woven out of bark fiber, these net bags are incredibly strong, but I'd never seen a full-grown adult carried in one.

143

In a feat of strength and persistence, a young Moi man carried
the sick woman up the side of the mountain in a *noken*.

In the doorway of the aircraft, with a load of *kayu masohi*
in the background, Piato prays for the desperately ill woman
we're about to medevac to the hospital.

This dear woman is in obvious pain. Unable to walk, covered in soot, and wearing only a grass skirt, she's a picture of misery. She carries the image of her Maker and is a picture of one of "the least of these" that Jesus called us to seek out and love.

We lift her up into a seat, and as I get things ready to go, I notice that it's gone quiet on the opposite side of the airplane. I walk around to the other side and find Piato earnestly communing with his Creator, asking for healing for this desperately ill woman. No one asked him to pray. None of us "professional" Christians had gotten around to doing it ourselves yet. Piato just wanted to pray. Spontaneous. Natural. It was just what occurred to the former killer to do.

I'm thinking, *Look at this man who once killed so easily now praying so easily.* The transformation still stuns me. A violent man encounters Jesus and becomes a man of peace, a man of prayer.

Forgiveness. Redemption. Transformation. Jesus has brought all these things into Piato's life. And this is surely true for the rest of us. As you and I continue to cultivate our own encounters with Jesus, he'll continue transforming us into beautiful reflections of himself

The quote at the chapter head is from a column in *The Times* UK newspaper, December 27, 2008.

33

WHERE I COME FROM

God takes pleasure in disappointing their expectations
who promise themselves great things in the world,
and he delights in outdoing the expectations
of those who promise themselves but a little.

—MATTHEW HENRY

Nate, age 4, joining in the rice-threshing process
in the village of Bokraha, Nepal, ca. 1972

For a couple of years, I used the above picture as the desktop background on my computer. I put it there so that every day I would see it and remember where I come from. A couple of my friends thought it was to remind myself of the days when I still had hair. What do they know? This was the Kurukh village of Bokraha, in the Terai region of southeast Nepal where we lived much of the time in my early years.

For me, as a kid, life was good. I remember being able to get through my schoolwork by late morning (it was that, or Mom just wanted me out of the house), and it was off to the great outdoors for the rest of the day.

Life was simple. Our home had mud walls (really) and a thatch roof. And while that may sound pretty rough, we were actually raising the bar for remote village living by having running water *in* our house. This consisted of a single pipe sunk straight into the ground, topped off with one of those old-fashioned cast-iron, hand-operated water pumps. Boom, *indoor* plumbing. Pretty sure Dad took some flack from some of the more hardcore missionaries for this extravagant luxury.

If my memory serves me correctly, the extent of my toys in Bokraha was a bunch of marbles, whose quantity varied based on how well I was doing in the daily cutthroat games on the packed dirt at the village center. In addition, I was fortunate enough to have among my possessions an eight-inch iron hoop, which provided countless hours of fun. We would run along the top of the narrow paths on the rice paddy dikes at a full gallop, using a stick to push the iron ring along in front of us. You had to be there.

When you got bored of the hoop and the marbles, you could always smack the backsides of the cows with a stick to keep them moving around the threshing floor.

It is largely due to the circumstances of my childhood that I now live with an almost perpetual sense of wonder … amazement that my world ever morphed into something more than marbles, iron rings, and whacking cows' butts. On days when I lose that wonder, I lose my joy. If I remember where I've come from, I pinch myself and am awed anew that I've traded in the rebar ring for a 33-year-old rusty Landcruiser that starts almost every morning. This makes me ask the Lord *why me*

Nate with his parents, Kent and Sandy Gordon, and his three
sisters, Becca, Meg, and Sarah (left to right), in the village of
Bokraha, Nepal, ca. 1975. "If I had to guess, I think I'm the only
one of us four kids wearing shoes because I was about to go on
a trip with my father on the motorcycle."

questions, such as: *Why, with all the things that can go wrong in life, do I
have it so good?*

If I've lost that wonder, then I'm miffed because of the muddy water
on my shoes from the puddle I just drove through, and I start asking the
Lord a different set of *why me* questions. Questions such as: *Why do I
have to have a car with holes in the floor?*

When I think about it, where I truly come from is a place of great
need. I should spend each day in wonder that Jesus has answered that
need by picking up the filth of my sin, having it slop all over him, and
then, guilty of having my sin on his hands, he's executed in my place.
Then he returns somehow more alive than before, and, with a smile,
points at the narrow way and says to me, "Follow."

And in awe I ask, "Lord, why me?"

34

HOUDINI PIG

No ropes or chains can keep me from my freedom.
—HARRY HOUDINI

It's 8:00 a.m. and I'm in my second village of the day, the Ketengban community of Okbap, 6,000 feet above sea level in Papua's Star Mountains. On the way in, Okbap's radio operator asked me to do a shuttle over to the large government center at Oksibil. I agreed to help them out. I'll take some passengers to Oksibil and, once there, pick up a load of medicine to bring back for the community clinic at Okbap.

Because the clock is ticking towards the 10:00 a.m. wind curfew at Okbap, I've got to keep things moving. A bunch of strong Ketengban guys jump into action to help me load the airplane at Okbap. We stick a very large and very dead pig in the back, and then throw in the passengers' baggage: an assortment of ten or fifteen nokens full of sweet potatoes, fruit, pots and pans... Honestly, I was in a hurry and didn't pay too much attention to the content of the nokens—just standard Papuan baggage.

I get the passengers in their seats and their seatbelts buckled. One passenger will sit beside me up front, and the remaining three on a bench seat directly behind me.

We're airborne after a short takeoff run down the 20% slope, which the people of Okbap have carved out of their mountain to serve as the community's airstrip. Soon I'm at 9,500 feet, negotiating the Abmisibil Pass. The wreckage of a Twin Otter on the mountainside passes by on our left.

The smooth morning air is suddenly shattered by a shock wave of turbulence. I yank the power back to slow the airplane down, and take a glance behind me to make sure my passengers are still in possession of their breakfasts. To my horror, where there were three passengers, there are now only two. I'm getting old and forgetful, but I could have sworn I took off with three people in that seat. Yes, in fact, I remember now, the passenger in the middle was a little old woman. She's gone. As I'm beginning to think through how on earth I'm gonna explain this one to the safety committee, a wizened little head pops up from behind the bench seat and gives me a broad smile. The incredulity on my face must have translated, and one of the guys still in the seat yelled to me above the noise, "A pig got loose, so she went back there to hold on to it." It seemed to him a perfectly reasonable thing to do.

"Get back in the seat and put your seatbelt on!" She might not be so lucky on the next jolt of turbulence. She quickly clambered over the seat with a dexterity that I'm sure I will not possess when I'm her age.

Granny is secured. Houdini the pig is still on the loose. In the 5 minutes before landing at Oksibil, I cast numerous glances behind me to check on footloose Granny and to make sure that Houdini wasn't committing any mischief. At this point, I hadn't seen the critter, but I knew he couldn't be too big because the really big one was dead, which meant Houdini had to have been in one of the nokens that had been tossed in the back under the cargo net.

After landing, I hopped out and quickly went to the back of the airplane to meet the author of all our troubles and found that Houdini was a tiny tike of a piglet. He was standing on the wrong side of the cargo net looking guilty. I have no idea how he got out of his noken but, once out, it was an easy thing for him to get through the wide webbing of the cargo net.

Houdini pig

All's well that ends well, I suppose. As I got out my all-purpose rag to clean up a mess on the cabin floor, I thought to myself that at least the turbulence hadn't scared my passengers that much. The pig was the only one whose bladder had committed an indiscretion.

35

MUCH AFRAID

Death is not the worst of evils.
—GENERAL JOHN STARK

Fear strikes me as one of the most profitable psychological responses God has given us. I can't imagine trying to cope in this broken world without it. As an aviator, fear often keeps me from doing something really stupid. The mountains of Papua are littered with the wreckage of aircraft whose pilots were unafraid when they desperately needed to be terrified.

But it also seems to me that our emotions, corrupted by the fall, don't always serve us in the way they were designed to. And so, I end up fearing the wrong things.

Take people, for example. I'm not afraid of people. Except when I am. If I'm not walking in communion with God, I'm far too concerned about what people think of me. I particularly don't like it when folks are mad at me or, worse, have a firm conviction that I'm an idiot. Fearful of these things, I tailor my actions to avoid anger and ridicule. The irony is, I may actually do the right things, but I'm motivated by the wrong thing: fear of man.

Jesus gives us some explicit guidance on fear. Apparently, there are things that we should fear, and things that we should not. Like the prudent aviator, fearing the right things will keep us from doing something stupid with catastrophic consequences.

Luke records these remarkable words from our Master:

I tell you, my friends, do not be afraid of those who kill the body
and after that can do no more.

Jesus spoke these words to a group of men who, by their association with Jesus, had ticked off some really important people. These guys were keenly aware that there was a demographic who would love for them to be dead, and they had no friends in high places to help them. That was their context. My context? Well, I know a few folks who are not exactly fond of me, but I don't believe that anyone's out to put arsenic in my tea. For Jesus and his early followers, most of the people with real power were wholly committed to doing them grievous bodily harm. Jesus tells his friends that all these supposedly powerful people can do is kill the body ... *and after that can do no more.*

Profound. Jesus is saying that *the very worst thing that another human being can do to me really isn't that bad.* This is absolutely liberating, *if* we see things as Jesus does: That this life is not all there is. That I'm temporarily trapped in a broken place that is groaning for renewal. That our lives here on earth are but a vapor that passes quickly. If I'm able to see that my death will be followed by life as it was originally designed by our Creator, redeemed back to the beauty, peace, and happiness of the original design.

If we can see these things, *who, then, shall we fear?*

If the *who* is limited to our fellow human beings, then the answer that Jesus gives us is, clearly, no one. Even if they purpose to kill you. It would seem, then, that we should be fearless, and that fear itself is more or less a nuisance. But Jesus doesn't give us time to let the mortar of that musing harden. He immediately continues this amazing Luke 12 discourse with these words:

But I will show you whom you should fear:
Fear him who, after your body has been killed,
has authority to throw you into hell.
Yes, I tell you, fear him.

So, fearing the appropriate things: this is wisdom. I think the Bible even says so somewhere. But many of us in Western Christianity have muzzled Jesus on this score. In the sermons we hear or the books we read, how often are we loved enough by our teachers to hear these life-giving words of Jesus? We have made God into an image to our liking, and he is not a God to fear. We have made him a God for us to love and a God for us to be loved by. Full stop. We like our one-dimensional God.

But almost nothing about God, nor anything that he has created, is one-dimensional.

Take waterfalls, for example.

It's really not fair… I get to fly over some of the most majestic waterfalls on the planet. The mountains of Papua are literally covered with the things. There is so much rain here that almost every mountain has dozens of huge waterfalls cascading over its cliffs. Some of them are so isolated that I'm convinced no human being has ever stood at their base, soaking in their beauty.

I love waterfalls. They fill me with a fairytale sense of wonder. Their pure beauty creates an immediate peace in my soul. They remind me of all that is good in the world. I cannot fly by one without these wonderful emotions rising within me.

But waterfalls are terribly dangerous things. Our home in Papua is at the foot of Mount Cyclops. We can sit in our living room and take in the view of the mountain and its picturesque waterfall. And yet, a missionary died climbing that pretty waterfall.

When our son, Cameron, was three, I almost lost him in a gorgeous, terrifying Papuan waterfall. For six months afterwards, I would wake up in the middle of the night with a start, heart racing as my dreams had taken me back to that awful struggle against the current to reach my son, as a beautiful wall of water did its best to drown him. I almost lost that struggle. I love waterfalls. I fear waterfalls.

And God is much the same way. Beautiful. Lovely. Easily worshiped. Brings us a great sense of peace, and, yet, he is also a force greatly to be feared.

Yes, I tell you, fear him.

And if you fear him, you live in such a way that you enjoy his wonder, beauty, and love, and, fearfully, you are driven to obedience by a respect of this majestic force. You listen and obey when you hear his Spirit saying things like, "There's a line here. Don't cross it. Don't jump in so close to the waterfall's base. It can kill you."

Jesus knew our psyches well. He was all too familiar with our silly compulsion to categorize people, and even God, into one-dimensional categories. He tells us unflinchingly to fear God. But I have a feeling that he knew that if he left it at that, we'd have all died of our ulcers. He pushes another dimension of God on us. He immediately follows "fear him" with these incredible lines:

Are not five sparrows sold for two pennies?
Yet not one of them is forgotten by God.
Indeed, the very hairs of your head are all numbered.
Don't be afraid; you are worth more than many sparrows.

Peace.

36

Eden Leaking Through

Humility is walking throughout life
with this profound realization every day:
God has given me a lot more than I deserve.
—Dr. Kevin DeYoung

I'm sitting on the dunes at the edge of Michigan's Grand Traverse Bay, worlds away from the ministry in Papua. Waves gently lap the shore. The sun is just starting to come up behind me. I can feel its gentle warmth on my shoulders. The ripples on the water dance in that magical light of a brand-new day. I wonder why it is that God has allowed so much of the original wonder that he created on this planet to filter through the thick fog of sin. We have badly broken this place, and it seems to me that God should have abandoned us to our own devices, with the natural consequence that complete chaos and brokenness become the absolute rule. A kind of permanent post-nuclear winter from the fallout of the sin-bomb. And, truthfully, to a large extent, that is true of the world. Yet there are still moments of beauty, tranquility, and peace. Like this one.

As I walk out to the water's edge, two young rabbits hop themselves out of my way. A pair of mallards float peacefully in the shallows. The sun is warming my back, and it feels almost personal. The wild flowers that crest the tips of the grasses on the dunes display a beauty that seems wasteful and extravagant. Grass, this beautiful? Why?

The wildflowers, on the shores of Michigan's
Grand Traverse Bay, that sparked the thoughts in this chapter

When I approach life as though I still live in Eden, I am disappointed and deeply unsatisfied. There's just too much evidence to the contrary. Too many disappointments. Too many broken things. Too many broken people. Too much broken me.

When I see this world as a post-atomic rubblescape that should hold nothing but despair and yet instead holds these occasional moments of quiet peace, beauty, and wonder, I'm satisfied, content, and awestruck at how unfair it is that, though we pulled the trigger and devastated this place, God still allows so much of his original creative plan to leak through onto our landfill. And what leaks through from the original Eden is often so unspoiled and pure. Like these wildflowers.

Why the wildflowers, God? Perhaps you want us to glimpse a bit of heaven, and hunger for it. Too often, though, we see this place as heaven and, even though we have a sense somewhere in our souls that it just can't be, we try to structure the hell out of our lives and orchestrate 24/7 heaven on our broken planet. The amazing thing is how close some of us come to achieving just that. And then along comes cancer, and the

160

landfill snaps back into focus. It seems to me that I should be living with a worldview that expects cancer, and along comes a simple sunrise that shatters, for a moment, my worldview of brokenness.

And in that moment, I'm reminded that the world of pain is temporary and that Eden is coming.

Come quickly, Lord Jesus.

37

A MUCH HARDER THING

*If there was an easier way, you better believe
Jesus would have been the first to tell you.*
—Dallas Willard

I came to the story of the rich young guy in Luke 18, and, honestly, I breezed right through it because I had been through Matthew's account recently. But after skimming the story, I forced myself to read it again, and a couple things caught my eye.

You know the story: rich guy comes to Jesus wanting to know what he needs to do to "inherit eternal life." Jesus gives him a tract with the four spiritual laws. Oops, sorry, that's what *we* do. Jesus, on the other hand, completely forgets everything he learned in Sunday school and answers our man's question by telling him he needs to, get this, *obey the law*. Let's google it: see if we can find me a modern evangelism course that starts off by teaching people they need to obey the Ten Commandments. And yet this is exactly what Jesus does.

Honestly, I don't have this one figured out. But while it gives me significant pause, it didn't bother our rich guy one bit—he's got this Ten Commandment stuff in the bag and he tells Jesus as much.

Jesus doesn't dispute his claim to having been a good boy. He simply adds one more thing for the rich man to do. And this one thing puts the kibosh on his whole get-into-heaven quest. But wait, is it one thing that Jesus asks of him, or two? Jesus tells him,

Sell everything you have and give to the poor,
and you will have treasure in heaven.
Then come, follow me.

My guess is that Part One—the garage sale idea—was enough to derail our guy. Getting any of us to part with our filthy lucre is a pretty tall order, and the more we have of it, the more attached to it we tend to be. But I really wonder what might have happened if Jesus had left it at that—just get rid of your stuff, and you're good to go. Here we have a rich guy in complete control of his life. If all Jesus gave him was Part One, and our rich guy managed to pull it off, then all we'd end up with is *a poor guy in complete control of his life.* To me, Part Two—*follow me*—is the much harder thing.

Part One is expensive.

Part Two is ruinous.

Part One bankrupts your wallet.

Part Two bankrupts your self-determination.

Jesus' followers didn't just stick a "follower of Jesus" statement on their blog and get on with life. They left their lives behind and started new ones where they were simply, um, followers. We use this word so much we need to pause and meditate on what it means to be a follower of someone else. You go where he goes. You sleep where he sleeps. You eat what he eats. You pitch your rugged individualism off a rugged cliff.

And being a follower makes you weird. You become an eccentric, even within the community of people who are pursuing God. It's one thing to pursue God. Quite another to follow him. You pursue him on your own terms. You follow him on his. Pursuing God is a generally respectable activity. Following him earns you sympathetic glances.

And this is the essence of my struggle. Am I really following Jesus? Or am I on my own journey? Does he really lead me, and do I follow wherever his path may lead? Or am I staying within the well-drawn lines of what the current iteration of Christian culture determines to be adequate for a pursuer of God?

Keeps me up at night, frankly.

38

LIFE IS TERMINAL

The sweetest thing in all my life has been the longing ...
to find the place where all the beauty came from
—C.S. LEWIS

Recently, Sheri and I spent part of an afternoon walking through an ancient cemetery in Stark, New Hampshire. We wandered through the markers, reading the names, while a warm wind blew through the tops of huge pines. Some folks didn't make it to their ninth birthday. Some lived into their 90s. Some of the gravestones, dated in the mid-1800s, were so weatherworn they were hard to read. Some markers were brand new. Some people, judging by the size of the rocks stuck in the ground, were wealthy. Some were poor. Some were kids. Some were soldiers. All their lives had one thing in common: they ended.

Why is it that the only thing I know with absolute certainty will happen to me I spend so little time thinking about? I know almost nothing about the future, but, intellectually at least, I *know* my days are numbered. But my response to that knowledge isn't what it should be, I think. If I knew for certain that a stock was going to rise 400 percent, I think I'd probably spend some time rearranging my meager resources to try and make them a little less meager. Knowledge of the future influences our actions today. Yet, there's only one thing I know for sure will happen in the future, and I hardly let it have any influence on my day-to-day activities.

Life on this planet is terminal.

To be a little more precise, life in the skins we're in is temporary. Life itself isn't temporary, only our skins are.

As I've previously written, when explaining death to my son, Cameron, when he was four, I told him,

Cameron, you will always be.
But someday, your body is going to stop working.

And I think this sense of continuity is what brings the proper perspective to death. J.R.R. Tolkien blessed us with a few profound sentences when, at a particularly dire point in one of his stories when there was almost certainly no hope, Gandalf turns to Pippin and says,

The journey doesn't end here.
Death is just another path; one that we all must take.

So, I live my life here with the knowledge that my days on this planet are limited. My opportunities to fully submit and follow hard after God, in this place, are numbered. I can tread water until that day when my body quits, living an average life, on a pleasant path of my own choosing. But what an opportunity I have to make the most of these short days to enjoy the adventure of following him fully.

***

I wrote the preceding piece on September 18, 2011. Four days later I woke up to the news that one of our pilots, my good friend Paul Westlund, had perished in an aircraft accident in the mountains of Papua.

My stunned spirit wrestled greatly with whether I actually believed the stuff I'd just written. It's either true or it's not, and there's nothing in my world with more significant implications.

I believe, Lord. Help my unbelief.

39

PAUL

If you're breathing, you should be laughing.
—PAUL WESTLUND

One of God's greatest gifts to his followers are the encouragers he sends us. On September 22, 2011, the body of Christ lost one of God's gifted encouragers. My friend and fellow pilot Paul Westlund perished in an aircraft accident, along with his two Papuan passengers. As I write these words, two months after the fact, my heart still experiences seasons of heavy grief. We do not grieve as those who have no hope, but we do grieve. I ache for Paul's wife, Lavonne, their grown daughter, Joy, and their teenage son, Mark.

As God now has Paul with him, I suppose there's some danger that those of us left behind will glorify the person and let God be lost in the accolades for the one he created. But God also gave us each other to "spur one another on toward love and good deeds," and as I remember Paul, that is exactly what my spirit is longing to do: follow the example that Paul set for me in so many ways.

Paul was, without question, the most encouraging person I've ever been around. God would plant harebrained ideas in Paul's head about how to love on someone and, unlike me, Paul gave the matter no further thought: he simply went out and did it. He would walk into my office

It was hard to catch Paul Westlund without a smile on his face.

with no other purpose than to say a kind word to me … and then, as abruptly as he'd entered, he'd leave.

I worked with Paul for fourteen years. We spent countless hours together in the cockpit—he was at my side when God led us to the missing aircraft (see chapter 19, "A Missing Aircraft"). I can say, without hesitation, that he was one of the most upbeat and carefree people I've ever known. One of his favorite parts of the life God gave him was participating in the celebrations when a people group received God's Word in their language for the first time. At the celebration Paul would always get a copy of the newly printed Scriptures and begin asking everyone he came upon and to read his favorite verse. Then he'd have them sign their names in the front of the Bible.

Paul's favorite verse? 1 Peter 5:7

Cast all your anxiety on him because he cares for you.

Paul's unflagging carefreeness came from having a lock on that amazing truth that *God cares for us*. And what a gift that promise is to those of us left behind.

At Paul's request, these Bauzi men read 1 Peter 5:7 to him the day
they received the New Testament in their own language.
(Photo courtesy of Tim Harold)

As I mentioned in the previous chapter, four days before Paul died, I
had written the following:

*So, I live my life here with the knowledge that my days on this
planet are limited. My opportunities to fully submit and follow hard
after God, in this place, are numbered. I can tread water until that
day when my body quits, living an average life, on a pleasant path of
my own choosing. But what an opportunity I have to make the most
of these short days to enjoy the adventure of following him fully.*

Paul fully enjoyed the adventure that God laid out for him. He was
just your average American, living an average American life, when a man
walked into the motorcycle shop where he was working and challenged
him to follow God into a life of missionary service. Paul didn't give the
matter another thought. He dropped his tools and followed Jesus down
the path.

How about you? Is Jesus calling? Are you giving it thought? Or, are you, like Paul, ready to drop everything when the Master calls and follow him?

The path ahead? Who knows? That's what an adventure is all about. You're following Jesus, not blazing your own trail. His path is one of satisfaction, significance, and a deep sense of meaning in a broken and chaotic world.

I'm convinced that God is calling more Paul Westlunds out from among his people. Don't turn away in sadness like the rich young ruler. Take a deep breath, get off your path, take Jesus' hand and follow him.

40

LIVE FREE OR DIE

He is no fool who gives what he cannot keep
to gain that which he cannot lose.
—JIM ELLIOT

Whenever we've returned to the United States between stints of service in Papua, we've been extremely fortunate to spend time in northern New Hampshire where my parents live. The area has an abiding sense of honor for the early leaders of this country. The mountains that dominate the views are named Washington, Jefferson, Adams, and Madison. New Hampshire's motto isn't some catchy new hook to pull in tourists. When you see a New Hampshire license plate, you're looking at words that were penned over two hundred years ago by a guy named General John Stark, one of the area's Revolutionary War heroes.

Live free or die.

That'll attract the pleasure-seekers.

Actually, from a license-plate-motto perspective, it gets worse because we're not getting the half of it. Stark's full statement, sent in a message to encourage his fellow patriots, was:

Live free or die. Death is not the worst of evils.

171

Death is not the worst of evils. Now there's a cheerful little ditty for your license plate.

But is it true? Are there worse evils than death? When I got the news that Paul had died in a crash, his death felt like the deepest of evils. And, in one sense, it was. God's original design didn't have death in the picture, and when he restores all things, we return to that original design and death goes away once again. Death entered the picture as the natural consequence of sin corrupting and destroying the paradise God created on this planet. In the wake of a sudden and tragic death, I can hardly imagine even the most hardened atheist not resonating with the feeling that something is dreadfully wrong here. *This isn't supposed to happen.*

And that's true; death isn't supposed to happen. We were designed for life, not death. This is why it is such *good news* that God gives us a way back to what we were designed for: *life.* Abundant. Eternal. And because I know somewhere deep in my soul that Paul is finally enjoying life as it was originally meant to be, his death doesn't feel evil any longer.

In the hours after I got the news, it shames me to admit that my courage, faith, and motivation deserted me like fair-weather friends. I wanted to quit. The costs were simply too high.

Through a process of time and gentle mercy, God brought Sheri and me to a place (as per usual, she got there first) where we could recount the cost, stare the risks in the face, and feel a wonderful peace. It is a peace that comes from seeing Jesus standing on the path, beckoning us to follow him, and realizing there is no other place we'd ever want to be than hand-in-hand with him on the path of his choosing.

General Stark was right, death is not the worst of evils. To allow fear, unbelief, and discouragement to push us off his path—that would be a triumph of evil much worse than death.

41

CLARITY

I have never had clarity; what I have always had is trust.
—MOTHER TERESA

Am I comfortable with paradoxes? Mystery? Having things in life that are unknowable? Not being able to understand all the reasons for why things happen?

I can't tell you the number of times clouds blocked my vision while flying, preventing me from seeing where I was planning on going. Sometimes clouds will block the mouth of a valley I need to enter to get to my destination. It wasn't uncommon, especially in the early morning, to have just a small wisp of mist float across a critical point on a final approach to a mountain runway, preventing a landing. In my early years of flying in Papua, I was prone to being frustrated by these ill-timed obstructions to my vision. With time, it became easier to trust the mists in my path as part of God's unfolding plan for the day.

The Apostle Paul had a lock on the truth of the gospel ... but he also recognized that we've been given only so much. Sometimes, clouds block our vision. Mystery, wonder, paradox, and unanswered questions float through our lives like a mist moving over the calm of an early morning lake... or a lone cloud blocking the entrance to a valley.

Of what we are able to see, Paul said,

For now we see only a reflection as in a mirror.

When the ethicist and philosopher John F. Kavanaugh went to work for three months at the "house of the dying" in Calcutta, he was seeking a clear answer as to how to spend the rest of his life.[17] On the first morning there, he met Mother Teresa. She asked, "And what can I do for you?" Kavanaugh asked her to pray for him.

"What do you want me to pray for?" she asked. Without hesitation, he asked her to pray for what had been weighing on him throughout his long journey from the United States: "Pray that I have clarity."

She answered, "No, I will not do that." When he asked her why, she said, "Clarity is the last thing you are holding on to and must let go of." When Kavanaugh commented that she always seemed to have the clarity he longed for, she laughed and said, "I have never had clarity; what I have always had is trust. So, I will pray that you trust God."

Trust the God of the mists.

---

17 As told in Brennan Manning's *Ruthless Trust: The Ragamuffin's Path to God* (HarperCollins, 2002).

42

THE GIFT

Don't judge each day by the harvest you reap
but by the seeds that you plant.
—ROBERT LOUIS STEVENSON

Returning to Papua, after losing Paul four short months earlier, was like returning to a childhood home and finding it different than you had remembered. The place was familiar, but nothing felt the same. I found myself wondering if I'd still have the joy that I'd had in the past, if fear would gain a foothold, and if the team would be the same without Paul's always-smiling, encouraging spirit.

God, in his mercy, didn't make me wait long for answers. My first flight back in Papua was a pure gift. Another of our pilots, Mark Hoving, was assigned to fly with me to knock off eight months of accumulated rust from my flying skills. We set out from Sentani in the early morning with four passengers. Our first stop was the village of Dofu, a red dirt hillock sticking out of the vast swamp 200 miles to our west. There, we dropped off two of our passengers: Jerrett Roy and Courtney Zehr, two pilots from our team, who were going to hop in a canoe and head downriver to the village of Wahuka to help Isolde, a 50-something German widow-turned-missionary to the Kirikiri people.

After bidding the guys a safe trip, Mark and I piled back into the airplane with our two remaining passengers. Steve and Carolyn Crockett were returning to the Moi tribe in the X-Ray valley to teach the Moi believers the newly translated book of 1 Corinthians. Steve tells me the timing is perfect: the young Moi church is facing many of the same issues that faced the first-century church in Corinth.

On the ground in Daboto, there's a warm reunion with Piato and the rest of the Moi. Among the crowd at the airplane are two patients. One, a pregnant woman who can barely walk, is doubled over in pain. Another is a young boy whose urine looks like pure blood (most likely a complication of malaria called blackwater fever). We fly these two to the coastal town of Nabire for medical help. Within the week, I've received word that they are both doing much better.

While refueling in Nabire, we meet up with the next leg of today's mission: a team of Papuan pastors and a load of their supplies, heading to Dofu. As we review our pre-start checklists, we hear the guys quietly praying in the back. These humble pastors made a trip last year to the Dofu area and upon witnessing the destitute conditions of the people living up and down the Mamberamo River system, they returned to the city and moved the hearts of churches across huge denominational boundaries to help alleviate some of the suffering they saw. Now, with over 1,000 pounds of supplies donated by these churches, they are returning to retrace their steps on the river to minister to the isolated peoples of the Mamberamo. To see such passion and commitment among Papuan pastors, sacrificially following Jesus on a very difficult mission, is humbling and exhilarating.

After saying our goodbyes to the pastors in Dofu, Mark is already in the airplane, and I'm about to climb in, when a fellow comes running up to tell me that they've heard over the radio that there is a really sick man in the nearby village of Foitau. Can we help him? Some quick math tells us we have the fuel and daylight to pull it off, and 10 minutes later we're landing in Foitau. An emaciated old man staggers to the airplane with his adult son. I help him up into a seat, and as I grab his arms, I feel literally no muscle. Through his dry, worn-out skin my hand feels only the thin hard bone of his upper arm. I hope we're not too late.

Landing back in Sentani, I'm realizing what a gift this first flight back in Papua is to me. It's as if God wanted to leave me no doubt as to why we're here. A couple of our pilots are now out in the steaming jungle helping a German widow reach the Kirikiri people. The Moi believers are hearing 1 Corinthians for the first time. A pregnant woman, a sick little boy, and a deathly ill old man are all getting the touch of much-needed medical care. A group of national pastors is heading out into the wilds to minister physically and spiritually to some of the most isolated and forgotten people on the planet.

And all of this on a single flight.

I'd like to think we followed Jesus to this place regardless of whether we would see fruit in the ministry, so to see him work so clearly, in a single day, through a team of deeply flawed missionary aviators and their extremely limited resources, is simply a gift from God that fans our passion for being here.

43

IMPOSTERS

My deepest awareness of myself is that I am deeply loved by Jesus Christ,
and I have done nothing to earn it or deserve it.

—BRENNAN MANNING

I rarely learn anything of lasting value from success.

Not that success isn't an accomplished teacher; it's simply that she generally teaches me the wrong things. Victor Hugo wrote these profoundly insightful words:

Success is a very hideous thing.
Its false resemblance to merit deceives men.

Unfortunately, when I sit in the classroom of success, I'm quick to learn and easily deceived. After meeting with success in an endeavor, behind a humble face, my prideful heart learns the wrong things:

So, I am something special after all. At the very least, this finally proves that I'm better than that guy over there.

I'll betcha I can pull this off again. This time, since I now know what I'm doing, let's skip the whole prayer part.

People are giving me credit for this success. They can't all be idiots. Maybe it really was me that has made this happen?

This success kind of rebalances things for me, right? I don't really need to keep seeking God's help in those weak areas of my life. Success covers a multitude of sins.

Wow, is applause ever underrated! Who knew? I could get used to this. Let's see, what could I do to top that last act?

Spiritually, I've learned far more from my failures than from my successes. Defeat tends to keep me humble, teachable, broken, and dependent on my Creator. In the past, I've told guys I've been mentoring that, spiritually, *success is your enemy; defeat is your friend.*

There's a lot of truth in that. We need not be terrified of defeat, and we need to be extraordinarily wary when we meet with success. Recently, though, I've been thinking a lot about how I can also learn the wrong things from failure. Kipling famously wrote in his poem "If—":

> *If you can meet with Triumph and Disaster*
> *And treat those two impostors just the same; ...*
> *Yours is the Earth and everything that's in it.*

Defeat is also an impostor, and we can learn the wrong thing from him.

For one, defeat does not necessarily mean you are on the wrong path. It could mean that you are smack in the center of the path that God wants you on. Neither does meeting with failure mean that God is displeased with you. It could mean that he didn't avert the current disaster precisely because he so delights in you. He's given you the gift of a failure to keep you close to him, to keep you from wandering off like I do when I encounter that other impostor named Success.

44

Choose Your Heroes Well

Think of no other greatness than that of the soul,
no other riches but those of the heart.
—John Adams

My boots were new, shiny, and, above all, dry. They recoiled at the sight of the massive mudhole that materialized out of the shadows on the trail ahead. Rats. But wait, this might be doable. I gingerly placed my steps on the few rocks that poked out of the muck. My friend Bram, who hails from Bandung in West Java, sloshed up from behind, laughing. "Give it up, Nate. You're going to spend the rest of the day with your feet in the water!" he said, happily plowing a wake through the mud.

Bram speaks truth. He's done this particular trek through the jungle countless times. We were slogging through a quagmire that, when dry, might have looked something like a trail. The muddy track paralleled crystal-clear waters of a jungle river flowing swiftly out of the Star Mountains. We wove our way between the huge trees that lined the river's banks. For the next five and a half hours, the only relief from the mud came when our feet found themselves in the pristine river. We crossed the torrent so many times I lost track. Each time, two sure-footed Papuans unobtrusively placed themselves on either side of me, waiting for me to fall. I didn't disappoint. My only source of pride was that, by swiftly sticking my arm straight up in the air, I always managed to keep my camera out of the water.

On the trail to Pipal. Our feet spent much of the day in water.

Tim Ruth and Bram Martin, happy warriors,
cross a shallow section of the river.

As it began to rain, Tim snapped this shot of the moment
we met Paulus for the first time.

For the last hour of the hike, we split off from the main river, but our soggy feet found no reprieve as we followed a smaller stream through a deep gorge. Finally, we left the wet behind and began climbing a steep mountain wall. Emerging at the top of the bluff, we saw what we had come to see: a 1,000-foot stretch of ground that, with immense toil, had been hacked out of the mountain, the rough shape of an airstrip. As I pulled out my inclinometer to measure the slope, Bram crested the cliff and stood beside me.

"Let's pray, Bram. If the slope here is greater than 15%, this won't work as an airstrip, and the people's incredible labor will have been for nothing." We talked to God for a moment. I feared the worst as I sighted the top of the airstrip. I showed the reading to Bram: 14%. He literally jumped up and down, shouting his joy. To ensure that our feet wouldn't dry out, it began to rain. We trudged up the slope of the airstrip towards the shelter of the lone hut where we would spend the night. An old man hobbled down the airstrip towards us. We met halfway and he embraced me, weeping. His name was Paulus (Paul). As we stood there in the rain, others surrounded us and they told me his story.

In 1977 Paulus set his people free. His people had never known anything but a fearful world controlled by powerful evil spirits and full of murderous enemies. That year, an entire village had been wiped out by a neighboring tribe. But in that same fateful year, Paulus and others heard of some very strange happenings several valleys to the south. Intent on seeing for himself, he left his area and hiked south through the mountains until he encountered a missionary who told of an almost-too-good-to-be-true path to relationship with the Creator. Somewhere in his soul, Paulus knew what he was hearing was true.

He stayed on in that foreign valley for some time, continuing to learn about this new path. Eventually he attended a newly formed Bible school there. He then hiked back to his area, bringing this good news with him. Paulus spent much of the rest of his life faithfully trekking throughout a wide area of mountains, rivers, and thick jungle, bringing this message that brought peace with God, peace with enemies, and freedom from the tyranny of the spirits. "He's the one who brought the gospel to us," the people told me.

"And now," he said to me through his tears, "I am old. But before I die, I have one last prayer, and that is that my home village, the most isolated of this area, would finally have an airstrip."

I turned to those standing near us. "Here is a real missionary if there ever was one. Someday we'll meet him again, and I think he'll be standing in a place of honor, next to the other apostle named Paul."

Choosing one's heroes is dicey, but I don't hesitate to call a guy a hero who has served God in complete anonymity in one of the harshest, most remote environments on the planet, eking out a living from his gardens and trekking weeks to bring peace and freedom to his enemies.

Then there's Bram. He comes from a Christian family 2,000 miles away on the island of Java. He felt God clearly call him to serve as a missionary in Papua. His family wouldn't hear of it. Even his church told him not to go. So, with no backing and $200 in his pocket, he left everything he knew behind for Papua and hiked into this remote area to love these people and teach them more about the God Paulus had introduced them to.

Bram and Paulus

The people of Pipal honoring Bram with a
bird of paradise headdress

"Matthew 6:33 is true, Nate. Four years later I still have that $200 in my pocket. God has provided for all my needs as I've served him out here."

Bram is the answer to Paulus' prayers and, humanly speaking, he's the reason that these people will get an airstrip. During our three days together in the jungle, I can tell that the love between Bram and the people of these mountains is mutual and genuine.

Our family, our church, and a host of friends stood solidly behind Sheri and me, encouraging us onward, when we left our country. Bram left his home in West Java with his church telling him he was doing the wrong thing, with his family hoping he'd soon run out of money and be forced to return home. Comparing ourselves to others is a generally unhealthy sport, but I can't help but be humbled by the contact I have with missionaries like Bram and Paulus.

That night I didn't sleep a wink, and it wasn't due to the cockroaches crawling all over me. ("Don't worry," says Bram, "if they crawl in your ears, I've figured out how to get them out. I shine a flashlight in there and they crawl out towards the light.") The people of this mountain are so excited by the news that the airstrip site will work that they dance all night.

All night.

Right outside our hut.

45

SWAPPING ADDICTIONS

Any man can stand adversity—
only a great man can stand prosperity.
—ROBERT INGERSOLL, SPEAKING OF ABRAHAM LINCOLN

Interesting little paragraph in John's twelfth chapter. Apparently, even some of the Jewish elite were overcome by the evidence and believed that Jesus was the Son of God. They got their feet through the door, then those feet got cold and they beat a hasty retreat to the known and the comfortable. John tells us that they knew that following Jesus would cost them their synagogue cards, so they kept quiet.

For they loved human praise more than praise from God.

Praise from men. We are absolutely addicted to it. And, like good junkies, we want our friends to be addicts too. When we find someone who in earnest doesn't care what the elite think of him, well, just one thing to do: rally the mobs and crucify him.

Praise from men. Its tentacles are so deeply wrapped around our souls I don't think that any of us can see how insidiously our motivations for doing the right things are corrupted by our heart's addiction to the praise of men. Why do we work so hard to prepare a great sermon? Why do we help the little old lady? Why do we lead worship? Why do we give to the poor? Why do we avoid external sin? Why do I write these words?

I'm afraid of the answers to those questions. Too many times the praise of men, at least in part, fuels my actions.

But hang on a second. There's something else here. John's words hold hidden treasure. These men loved the praise of men *more than praise from God.*

Praise from God? Is that possible? Can we even dream that the God who created the universe might find occasion to be pleased with us? Can we go there? What if we dared?

In daring, I find hope for my wandering heart and a breathtaking source of strength for obedience.

It seems that John would be telling us not only that praise from God is possible, but that we should love it. Pursue it. Crave it. Now here is something that can fuel a passion to follow Jesus even at great personal cost. The thought that by submitting to the Spirit of God, following where he leads, I can hear him say, "Well done!" This is nothing short of life-changing.

And, it might even be the way out of the praise-of-men addiction.

46

FREEDOM

Freedom?
Well, that's just some people talking.
—DON HENLEY, GLENN FREY

I am not a free man, but I wish to be.
Free of myself.
Truly free.

Free to live as a stranger in this world.

Free to be poor.

Free to be content.

Free to be self-forgetful.

Free to acknowledge my failures.

Free to return a blessing for a curse.

Free to be angry at the injustice others experience.

Free to love those who do not love.

Free to believe that prayer works.

Free to love my fellow man, not fear him.

Free to learn from those who oppose.

Free to be unknown.

Free to be unoffendable.

Free to walk in the opposite direction. Meekly.

Free to rejoice at the blessings others receive.

Free to have courage that fears God.

Free to weep with the pain others experience.

Free to work in obscurity.

Free to believe that God really can do the impossible.

Free to tell others about this Jesus, the One setting me free.

47

Heal Your Enemies

With Jesus, there is always hope.
—Debora Kagoya

A knock at the door.

"Mama, should we answer it?"

"Yes, children, answer it."

She'd been sick for over a month and hadn't been out of the house. Interethnic tensions in the community were higher than they'd ever been. People were being mysteriously killed. Everyone on edge.

"It's one of *them*," the kids told her. "Should we let him in?"

"Of course."

The man, a different race, a different religion, entered her humble Sentani dwelling.

"My child is sick. For five months we've done nothing but see specialists. She's still sick and our money is gone. We don't know where else to turn. Would you come pray for her?"

"Don't go, Mama!" The kids clung to her.

Deceit. Conspiracy. Treachery. Distrust permeated the atmosphere … and he was one of *them*.

"Live for God. Die for God." With these words she left her home and went with the man. For four days she prayed for his child. At the end of the fourth day, God healed the child.

"With Jesus, there is always hope," she told the father
and returned to her children.

*** *

We're rich. What else can I say? Every Sunday we sit in church and hear people stand up and share stories like this one told by a Sentani woman in obviously frail health.

I can't imagine two worlds more different than the world I see here, and the world Jesus saw around him in Palestine two millennia ago. But the words that he spoke on a hillside in Palestine are being followed by a few simple people out here in Papua, including a mother in poor health who is following this Jesus down a narrow path. He spoke on that hillside. He still speaks today. He says,

Love your enemies and pray for those who persecute you.

48

AMBITION

A man was meant to be doubtful about himself,
but undoubting about the truth.
—G.K. CHESTERTON

I was reading in Paul's letter to the Philippians this morning and was convicted again by these words:

Do nothing out of selfish ambition or vain conceit.
Rather, in humility value others above yourselves.

When is ambition not selfish?

I fear we have sanctified things that were never meant to be holy. Within the body of Christ do we even question ambition? Being upwardly mobile in ministry is an almost universal expectation and gets, at the very least, a complete pass and generally a wholehearted endorsement by the Christian community.

If ambition is selfish, then it is unholy. And I ask myself again, when is my ambition not self-centered?

From G.K. Chesterton's *Orthodoxy*:

Modesty has moved from the organ of ambition.
Modesty has settled upon the organ of conviction;
where it was never meant to be.

A man was meant to be doubtful about himself,
but undoubting about the truth;
this has been exactly reversed.

I believe every time I've seen those lines of Chesterton's quoted by a Christian author, the emphasis has been on the travesty of Christendom becoming modest about the truth. Fair enough. But Chesterton is also making the point that the Apostle Paul made: modesty and humility are to be what govern us, not ambition. We now read Chesterton's quote and don't even see this emphasis because self-promotion and the self-evident goodness of moving up in the world seem to be unquestioned givens.

I remember filling out a form for a Christian leadership seminar I was asked to attend. One of the first questions on the form was "What is your career goal?" This really threw me. Sanctifying the unholy?

As one who battles pride as much as the next guy, I still saw my life as one of following Jesus down a path of his choosing, not mine.

I wonder how much more powerful our ministries would be should modesty settle back on the "organ of ambition," and we refused to do its bidding any longer.

49

Eggs in a Thin Aluminum Basket

We are fragile creatures,
and it is from this weakness, not despite it,
that we discover the possibility of true joy.
—Archbishop Desmond Tutu

As I climbed up into the Pilatus Porter, I was warmed by the lighthearted chatter coming from the cabin behind me. The six guys in the back were ribbing each other with the ease that comes from decades of working together and perhaps from being well acquainted with each other's foibles. The easy goodwill and camaraderie were palpable. I smiled as I went through my pre-start checklists on the airplane. Andi, Demi, Yuli, Enos ... what a group of heroes.

Yapil was my last stop of the day, a day that felt a bit like driving the city bus. I'd been to the mountain villages of Kosarek, Nipsan, Omban, Okbap, and now finally Yapil. At these stops, I gradually collected the entire team of guys who have been working on the Ketengban Old Testament translation. As I started the airplane in Yapil, it dawned on me: I've got all the eggs in this basket. *Lord, we're always dependent on you for safety, but this would be particularly devastating to lose this group of men.*

As I thought about that flight, bringing the entire OT team out to Sentani for a couple of weeks of checking their drafts with their translation consultant, I was struck by an overwhelming sense of the tenuousness of our work. Suspended 10,000 feet up in an empty sky, a single engine pulling a pair of wings over a seemingly endless stretch of impenetrable rain forest … it was easy to feel incredibly vulnerable. All our eggs in a fragile aluminum basket.

Most of the time this endeavor of reaching the remotest parts of the earth with the good news of Jesus feels just like that: ridiculously fragile. The only way this work will ever succeed is if God undergirds it, protects it, and prospers it. It is, of course, *his* work, and it will bear fruit.

And the work, fragile and vulnerable as it may be, *is* bearing fruit. The Ketengban team we flew that day had a successful session of checking the Old Testament translation. A few short years later the Shorter Old Testament[18] was published in the language of their people.

---

18 Wycliffe Bible Translators, SIL International, the Bible societies, and other partners have together created a selection of Old Testament books and passages that make up the Shorter Old Testament, which the Ketengban translation team completed in 2014 and is being used by the church there. The Ketengban team then embarked on translating the entire Old Testament.

50

EVEREST

What we get from this adventure is just sheer joy.
—GEORGE MALLORY

Slowly, it materialized ahead of us in the clear mountain air. As we flew closer, the distinctive plume that streamed eastward from its summit left no doubt that we were looking at the highest mountain on the planet. Mount Everest framed in the windshield of a Pilatus Porter. Can this really be? I found it hard to believe.

Teammate Chris Jutte and I had come to Nepal to look at a Porter that was for sale. I had requested a short test flight over Kathmandu. Instead (long story), our short test flight turned into a never-to-be-forgotten foray to the flanks of Mount Everest, a low pass over the fabled Tengboche Monastery, and a delightful couple of hours in a tea shop in Lukla.

By God's grace, the deal went through, and we were able to purchase the aircraft for service in Bible translation in Papua.

Since its inception in 1959, Switzerland's Pilatus Porter has been inextricably linked to the similarly tiny, mountainous kingdom of Nepal. Pilatus conceived the aircraft specifically for high altitude, rough, unimproved airstrips, and they could think of no better place to prove the airplane than the roof of the world, in Nepal's Himalayan

Mount Everest as it appeared through the windshield
of the Pilatus Porter

mountain range. Indeed, the aircraft's name is a tribute to the famed
Sherpa porters who had made the conquest of Everest possible. And so,
in 1960, the very first Pilatus Porter out of the factory went to Nepal in
support of a Swiss climbing expedition, which ended up being the first to
reach the 26,795-foot summit of Dhaulagiri. (That aircraft still holds the
record for the highest altitude landing for fixed-wing aircraft at 18,865
feet on Dhaulagiri glacier—a feat that pilots still find astounding.)

Fifty-two years and 448 production aircraft later, I found myself at
the controls of the last Pilatus Porter to fly in Nepal. Five months after
that first trip to look at the aircraft, its wheels left the Nepali tarmac for
the last time, and I pointed her towards her new home. It was hard not
to feel a twinge of melancholy. And guilt. At least for the time being, the
Porter's remarkable service in Nepal had ended, and I was party to it.

The Porter's storied history in Nepal had overlapped my own in the
distant past as well. As a young boy, I'd seen Everest through the window of a JAARS-operated Pilatus Porter. My parents served as Bible
translators for the Kurukh people who lived in Nepal's lowland Terai

"I have a memory of seeing Everest through the window of
a Pilatus Porter when I lived in Nepal as a child. It was an
unexpected blessing to repeat that experience thirty years later."

region about 90 miles south of Everest, and I can clearly remember flights
with the entire vista of the Himalayas visible as we commuted between
Kathmandu and the village of Bokraha.

And so, it was with mixed feelings that we flew the last Porter out of
Nepal. The melancholy didn't last long. For one, my colleague Brad and
I were a mite busy steering clear of weather, mountains, and other airplanes as we exited the Kathmandu Valley to the southeast. We headed
out over the Terai and passed almost directly over that tiny village of
Bokraha where many of my childhood days were spent. Eight days and
5,000 nautical miles lay between us and home.

Low and slow, what a way to see Southeast Asia, and what a reminder
of the absolute magnificence of this world that God has created. Simply
awe-inspiring. It turned out to be the trip of a lifetime, and I can only
wonder, *Why me?* I can't answer that.

God overcame every single obstacle during the trip, giving us clear
paths through both the inevitable inclement weather and inclement

Brad McFarlane and Nate soon after arriving in Kathmandu
to ferry the aircraft back to Papua

Passing volcanoes on the island of Java in the early morning—just
one of the many incredible sights from flying low and slow across
Southeast Asia (Photo courtesy of Brad McFarlane)

bureaucracy we encountered along the way. We had the undeserved privilege to watch 6,000 miles of fabulously beautiful Asia pass below our wings (Nepal, India, Bangladesh, Myanmar, Thailand, Singapore, Malaysia, and the breadth of the Indonesian archipelago). Forty flying hours after departing Kathmandu, right on schedule, we touched down at the airport in Sentani, Papua. Tired, homesick, saddle-sore but exhilarated.

The aircraft is in Papua not because Brad and I brought it there, but because God's people parted with significant resources to purchase it. God's people purchased it so that we could use this tool to reach the 270 people groups isolated in the interior regions of Papua with the gospel of Jesus Christ and give them access to the riches of Scripture in their own languages.

Love Me.
Love people.
Use tools.
Don't get them mixed up.

51

NOTHING

If a man would make his world large,
he must be always making himself small.
—G.K. CHESTERTON

I've heard myself say that I want to be like Christ. The way those words roll easily off my tongue shows that, whatever my vague picture of being like Christ might look like, I'm probably thinking it's something I can pull off without breaking much of a sweat. If I'm honest, my concept of becoming more like Christ probably amounts to nothing more difficult than becoming a nicer person.

Sounds like an easily forgotten New Year's resolution. And it is.

Poking around in the letter that Paul wrote to the Philippian followers of Jesus, I start to feel like my stated desire to be more like Christ is actually a bit more like Peter's naive assertions that he would never deny his Master. Words spoken in good faith, but he simply did not know what he was talking about. And when I say that I want to be like Christ, I've not really grasped what is going to be required of me.

But fortunately, the Apostle Paul puts the cookies on the lower shelf in Philippians 2. With words inspired by the Creator, he tells me that my attitude should be the same as that of Christ Jesus. He then goes on to describe Jesus' attitude very clearly. And when I look at the description of what will actually be required of me to be like Christ, I realize that

I've had no clue what I've been talking about. My words have been empty and hollow. Like Peter, while my Master is laying down his life, I'm diligently trying to preserve my own, all the while thinking that I'm doing the right thing.

I don't come close to being like Christ because I've underestimated how different this Christ is from me and my culture.

Here's just one item from Paul's description of Christ: he tells us that Jesus

made himself nothing.

It's one thing to find yourself in lowly circumstances due to events beyond your control or as a consequence of your own action—both of which most of us have probably experienced. Once we've been forcibly taken to a lower station, it's not uncommon for followers of Jesus to then find the silver lining in the humility of a downgraded place in life.

But if we want to have the same attitude as that of Christ, we are instructed to follow his example and

make ourselves nothing.

This is another thing entirely. This means I am to actively seek the lower state. Get there under my own power. That's really, really hard. I can't remember ever doing that. In a world where doing what's right for yourself is not only the norm, it's almost considered a virtue, the concept of making intentional choices to go the other direction is beyond foreign.

And yet, there's this glimmer of the hint of tremendous treasure, hidden and waiting for the one who is willing to step off their own path and actually try to be like Christ Jesus, by making himself nothing.

52

BATS AND COCKROACHES, JUSTICE AND MERCY

Think carefully before asking for justice.
Mercy might be safer.
—MASON COOLEY

I was thinking about Micah 6:8 one evening and my thoughts kept being interrupted by the drumming wing beats of a fruit bat in full hover outside our window. That, and the cat, who was chasing a cockroach around the room for sport. Life is good. (The cockroach may beg to differ.)

I assume that Micah 6:8 was as beautiful in Hebrew as it is in English:

And what does the LORD require of you?
To act justly
and to love mercy
and to walk humbly with your God.

The prose can wander around my head for days just because it is so beautiful.

The prose can wander around my head for days without my head understanding what the prose actually means.

Justice and mercy are at odds with each other, aren't they? I mean, justice means making sure that a wrong doesn't go unpunished, and mercy means that, well, a wrong goes unpunished. So how do the two concepts end up right next to each other in Micah 6:8?

Not that these are foreign concepts to me. I know about justice and mercy, and it goes like this:

When I've done wrong, I want mercy.
When I've been wronged, I want justice.

Like so much else I learn from the Master, I find that my natural instincts are backwards.

The stress in Micah's words seems to be for a one-way justice—from me to others. *Act justly.* I think of Zacchaeus who paid back fourfold those he'd cheated. This is acting justly.

I think about Jesus having his beard ripped out by the roots while someone else's hot, hate-filled saliva runs down his face. *Love mercy.* He says not a word when he could have on the spot uttered the words to terminate his tormentors' existence. This is loving mercy.

Taking the prose to heart then, for me, means that it needs to go like this:

When I've done wrong, I will act justly.
When I've been wronged, I will respond with mercy.

When I step back and look at the broad strokes of how justice is portrayed throughout the riches of Scripture, from Micah to Jesus, it seems safe to say that we are to fight for justice for others and allow God to sort out justice for ourselves. My own Christian culture often seems to be pushing in the other direction: we fight for justice for ourselves and our own and let God sort everyone else out.

53

JESUS AT THE DOOR

Jesus is at the door, waiting for me.
I need to go.
—Zeth Nabyal

I had my flight helmet in my hand, walking out to the airplane to fly. Someone intercepted me as I neared the aircraft and delivered a bitter reminder of life's fragility. Good friend and colleague Zeth Nabyal had lost his short, terrible battle with tetanus.

Zeth left behind his wife, Selina, and their three beautiful children, Windy, Timothy, and Angely.

Through tears, Selina told Sheri and me that in the early morning Zeth had sensed it was time and told those with him,

I feel like this is the end.
Please pray for me.

One of the men in his hospital room began to pray. After a bit, Zeth interrupted him impatiently and said,

When are you going to get to "Amen"?
Jesus is at the door, waiting for me.
I need to go.

The man abbreviated his prayer. Then Zeth breathed his last ... and didn't keep his king waiting any longer.

Henry Moore invested many years in mentoring Zeth in the field of avionics (aircraft electronics), and Zeth served on our team in that capacity for more than fifteen years. But Zeth was so much more than a technician in the service of Bible translation. A pillar of his church, the chairman of the committee for translating the Old Testament into his native Una language, and a respected leader among the Una community, Zeth's presence here on this earth will be dearly missed by many.

Zeth is in heaven now. I think he may find it familiar. I will never forget the day when I sensed heaven come down and envelope Zeth and the other Una with him on a remote Papuan mountainside (see chapter 14, "Boxes").

Until we meet again, Zeth. Say hi to Paul for me.

Zeth Nabyal on the day his people received the
Scriptures translated into the Una language

54

Isn't *this* Worshiping God?

God has so arranged the world that work is necessary,
and he gives us hands and strength to do it.
—Elisabeth Elliot

We were midway through a pilot meeting when the door opened and two old guys walked in, unceremoniously interrupting the proceedings. Klaus Kugler, from Germany, and his American friend Jerry Reeder had a long history in Papua—they had begun serving here before some of the pilots in the room had been born.

Not all interruptions are created equal, and this one turned out to be quite magical. Jerry, in his younger years, had served in Papua as a missionary pilot. Klaus, after first working in Bible translation in Nepal, had come and served as a missionary among Papua's Fayu people, probably one of the most remote and isolated groups left on the planet. Many of the pilots in the room know Klaus, having flown him in and out of the Fayu area for years. Jerry is new to most of us. He makes his way to each pilot in the room, shakes hands and asks them to tell him a little about themselves. When he finishes, the retired, battle-tested pilot turned and addresses all of us,

You guys are the next generation.
Keep fighting the fight.

As the guy leading the meeting, I couldn't have scripted a more effective shot in the arm for our team. Just what we needed that day.

Klaus takes a turn to speak to the pilots. He points at me and says, "I knew this guy when he was just a kid in Nepal."

He gets teary.

"Nate's dad checked the first translation I ever did, the Gospel of Luke."

I get teary.

Klaus shares that he and Jerry have just come from a trip to Nepal. The tiny body of believers that Klaus knew when he left the country those many decades prior has done what followers of Jesus always do when they are persecuted: they blossomed. There are *one hundred* congregations in the people group now.

A few days after they crashed our meeting, one of our pilots flew Klaus and Jerry out to Fayu territory. The reception was enormous, deafening, total Fayu raucousness.

A week later, it's Saturday evening, and my phone is ringing. Jerry is desperately ill. Can we pull him out on Sunday? Fayu-land is so far from Sentani that we can't round-trip it without refueling, but I don't want to have to stop for fuel if Jerry is as bad as I'm being told.

Humanly speaking, YAJASI makes a difference at the end of the earth only because we've got a great team. Tonight, the team comes through. Sony and Jason give up a chunk of their Saturday evening to install the extra fuel tanks under the Porter's wings. In the dark.

It's still dark the next morning when my beat-up Landcruiser and I head to the hangar. I'm the last one to arrive. The team is already in high gear. Iput is finishing fueling the underwing tanks. Becca is on the radio, checking the weather at our destination—she'll stay and flight-follow us all morning. Yafet and Eko are tying down the load and getting the stretcher for me. The team is gung-ho, moving fast, and really kicking it getting the airplane ready. I thank the guys profusely for working on a Sunday morning. Quizzical, Yafet looks up from putting away extra cargo straps and asks, earnestly,

Isn't this *worshiping God?*

These brothers of mine get it much more than I do at times.

An hour and 45 minutes of seemingly endless rainforest puts me over the village of Dirouw. Moments after landing, Klaus is standing at my open cockpit door. His face is wan and strained. I can tell he's been through a tough 24.

"Nate, I am so glad to see you. I am so glad to see you. Yesterday, I thought I lost Jerry. He was totally unresponsive."

We get Jerry on the stretcher. The Fayu chief prays for him.

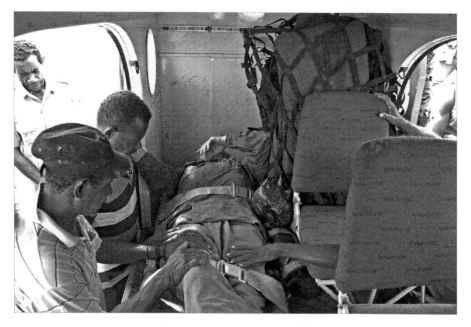

The Fayu chiefs praying for Jerry Reeder

Four days later I saw Jerry again. This time he was 100 percent vertical. Apparently, God listens to Fayu chiefs.

55

CLOSE TO DANGER, FAR FROM HARM

Faith ... makes nothing impossible
and renders meaningless such words as anxiety, danger, and fear.
—CHARLES DE FOUCAULD

The abrupt drop-off at the beginning of the airstrip flashed by a few feet beneath us. We were doing something like 65 mph. Just another normal landing at Langda.[19] For some reason though, on this day, the thought flashed through my mind that if, in that critical second, we bumped the power back ever so slightly, we'd land short of the airstrip and strew expensive aluminum all over the place.

Most of the time I don't think about stuff like that, but occasionally I have one of those hyper-aware moments when the reality of what you're doing snaps into uncomfortable focus. Like the fact that you're taking a 5,000-pound projectile freight-training along at 100 feet per second and attempting to slide it into a 100-foot box at the business end of a patch of ground carved out of no-nonsense jungle. Successfully pull that off and you find that the real fun is only just beginning. You now have to figure out how to corral the hurtling beast to a stop on a surface with the same consistency as the stuff escaping a 2-year-old's nose. And this corralling needs to be done with some dispatch lest you exhaust the snotty, but mercifully treeless, surface and slide off the far end of the airstrip into

---

19 We've been to Langda before, in chapter 14, "Boxes."

Approaching the cliff-edge end of Langda's runway is a bit like
landing on an aircraft carrier suspended 6,000 feet above sea level.

the no-nonsense jungle … and strew expensive aluminum all over
the place.

Draconian rules require that you keep your eyes open through the
entire process.

Life's a bit like that, too. Only, you're allowed to close your eyes. And
most of us do, creating the warm illusion of a safe and secure world
where danger resides far, far away somewhere on a CNN homepage.

The reality is, that once sin broke this incredible, used-to-be-perfect
place, death and danger became our constant companions. They are just
a bump of the throttle away.

But what if...

What if that which is most real, most valuable, and most desirable
to me is also totally secure and absolutely untouchable? What if no one,

no event, no circumstance, no illness, no *anything* can take away what is most important to me?

Ah, now danger still surrounds me, but harm?

I'm far from harm.

No matter what happens.

Even if the throttle gets bumped.

> *For I am convinced*
> *that neither death nor life,*
> *neither angels nor demons,*
> *… neither height nor depth*
> *nor anything else in all creation,*
> *will be able to separate us*
> *from the love of God*
> *that is in Christ Jesus our Lord.*
>
> —Romans 8:38–39

56

THE GARBAGE CHURCH

Our hearts of stone become hearts of flesh
when we learn where the outcast weeps.
—BRENNAN MANNING

The small group of believers we worship with is a motley crew of messed-up people if there ever was one. Any given Sunday sees the rough block building with the uneven cement floor and the cheap plastic seats filled with prostitutes, drunks, swindlers … and a bunch of the rest of us run-of-the-mill sinners. All in attendance are broken and in the process of being transformed by our encounters with Jesus. The pastor himself is an ex-drunk whom Jesus turned into one of the most passionate preachers I have ever heard.

Every Sunday we have an open mike testimony time, and it can be surreal. One of the women in the church shared that she had felt convicted to go and ask for forgiveness of the woman she had stabbed (for cheating with her husband). A young man shared recently that the reason he's there is because he'd seen the guy playing the bass guitar take a dramatic turn from a life of destructive sin to one filled with joy, purpose, a job, and family. He wanted his own life, currently caught in the self-destructive vortex of drugs/sex/drink, to experience the same change. Last week a woman asked for us to pray for her as she tries to reach out to the woman who is currently sleeping with her husband.

One of the leaders told us that some in town refer to the place as The Garbage Church. Human detritus washes up here. So much so that when the pastor saw our neatly dressed missionary family slip in the back for the first time, his shocked mind jumped to the logical conclusion: we'd gotten lost and wandered into the wrong place. Three weeks in a row, I've watched the same toddler pee smack in the middle of the center aisle while her barefoot mom looks on adoringly. The barefoot mom and her brood are fresh out of the jungle. Simple, uneducated, dirty clothes … and welcome here. Eventually they'll figure out there's an outhouse behind the church, but until then no one scorns them. After all, how much effort does it cost us to step across a puddle on our way to the front at offering time?

And it seems to me that Jesus actually goes out of his way to encounter the prostitutes, drunks, swindlers, and kids who pee on the church floor. He seeks out the broken. He doesn't seem much interested in those who think they're something special.

Been poking around the first book of Peter and have been hit by the words from Proverbs that Peter quotes towards the end of his writing:

God opposes the proud,
but shows favor to the humble.

Kind of lays out God's stance pretty clearly. If I am proud, the God who created the universe is in opposition to me. If I am broken, he's on my side.

What a gift to be surrounded by people who remind me to stay broken.

57

CHICKENS

*Happiness resides not in possessions, and not in gold;
happiness dwells in the soul.*

—DEMOCRITUS

Kept bumping into chickens the other day.

The first one was me. I've long tried to maintain the right dose of cowardice in my soul as it tends to aid longevity in this line of work. First landings at new airstrips may seem like the kind of thing missionary pilots live for and, to be sure, they are momentous occasions. But this particular missionary pilot is getting old enough that adrenaline has lost much of its novelty, and elevated risk gives me heartburn. That said, at some point somebody has to go break these places in, and so, after getting a good look at the airstrip via helicopter, it was time to go back into Pipal in something with wings attached to it.

Eight days after the helicopter foray, I was once again overhead Pipal. Mark Hoving was along as an extra set of eyes to help identify those "that looks dumb, let's not do it" scenarios.

We took our time flying test approaches and mapping out what altitudes to use over various landmarks along the approach path. The airstrip is located in a tight little box of a valley that allows you in, but at about a half a mile from touchdown, it becomes so tight that you can't turn around and get back out. We needed to make sure that we were spot-on when passing that point of no return.

On final approach for the first landing at the Pipal airstrip

After satisfying my inner chicken, we finally jumped in with both feet, flew past the committal point and landed. Parking on the tiny flat spot carved out at the top of the 15% slope, we were soon surrounded by a throng of Ketengban, dancing away in their Sunday best.

One thing you learn quickly about Papuans is that they really know how to party. I think Jesus feels so at home with them in that regard. They prepared a feast to mark the important day in their community's history, and Mark and I had the privilege of sharing it with them. Pigs are slow-cooked by super-heated rocks in a manner similar to a Polynesian luau. Tender and delicious. This is also where I met the second chicken of the day, cooked alongside its porcine brethren.

I'm privileged to know many followers of Jesus in the West who keep very loose hands on their possessions, giving generously. We operate millions of dollars' worth of aircraft that remind me of that fact every single day.

After the first landing, while the people of Pipal celebrated around
the aircraft, Paulus came to the door with a bird of paradise
headdress, which he put on Mark's head to honor and welcome him.

The airstrip at Pipal

The second chicken of the day

Papuan followers of Christ will not be outdone. As we were preparing to get back in the airplane to leave, Paulus, the man who has spent his life bringing the gospel to this remote area, presents me with the gift of a chicken (this one very much alive and feathered). When I think about the percentage of this man's material wealth that he gave me so freely, I am ashamed at how painfully I part with much, much less.

The third chicken of the day. Paulus demonstrates remarkable,
sacrificial generosity. (Bram at right)

As a filthy rich missionary by comparison, I could do nothing but graciously accept the incredible gift from my even richer brother ... who sleeps under a grass roof deep in the Star Mountains of Papua.

Has not God chosen those
who are poor in the eyes of the world
to be rich in faith
and to inherit the kingdom
he promised those who love him?

—James 2:5

58

MY BUCKET LIST

And people who do not know the Lord ask why in the world we waste
our lives as missionaries. They forget that they too are expending
their lives ... and when the bubble has burst, they will have nothing
of eternal significance to show for the years they have wasted.

—NATE SAINT

"I'm gonna add that to my bucket list..."

The fact that I think in these terms shows how prone I am to swallow concepts the world feeds me without much of a second thought. A second thought would, it seems to me, reveal that making a list of self-centered things to do before I kick the bucket is simply the current recycle of the "you only live once, pack as much in as you can" philosophy that sketches out the road map for the broad path. The whole idea runs squarely against the flow of Christ's lonely call for us to seek first his not-of-this-world kingdom ... and allow the Master to sort out which of life's amazing experiences he'll have us encounter along the narrow way.

And what happens if we ever get the list done? What then? Ever met anyone checking off the last box on their bucket list? I wonder what sentiment you would find there.

I once had the experience of witnessing a man check off the last box on his life's to-do list, though I'm positive he'd never heard of a bucket list.

With the first test landing successfully completed, the day came for the official opening of the airstrip at Pipal. We brought government inspectors in along with Bram and his mentor, Pak Aby. At some point in the festivities, Paulus says, in earnest,

Now I can die in peace.
The last thing that I have prayed that God
would allow me to accomplish—
the opening of an airstrip for my people—
is finished.

Having brought the gospel over the mountains for the people of this entire area, and having watched it begin to transform an entire culture, Paulus grieved that his home village remained without direct access to the outside world through an airstrip. This mission was the last thing he wanted to see happen before his waning years came to an end.

Now I can die in peace.

To die in peace. Now there's something worth adding to our lists.

And then I begin to wonder: how much different would our lives be if we made a list of things we wanted to happen *after* we kicked the bucket? Call it the post-bucket list.

On days when I'm able to keep what will happen after my last breath in view, even if it's just in my peripheral vision, well… those days are markedly different than when I'm simply striving towards something that won't outlast my own visit to this planet.

When I step back and set the goal of conducting the next hour of my life in such a way that I might hear "Well done!" from my Master, life takes on real meaning, is guided by purpose, and filled with peace.

59

FINDING ONYA

Little faith will take your soul to heaven,
but great faith will bring heaven to your soul.
—CHARLES SPURGEON

I got hung up on bucket lists for a spell. Seemed like everywhere I turned I was running into the phrase. Receiving an email from Andrew Sims, the man who has spent most of his life translating the Scriptures into the Ketengban language, there it was again:

Onya is a place I always had on my bucket list
but could never get there on foot.

Getting the airstrip open at Onya has been on my *own* list for some time. Now, with Ketengban Old Testaments piled high in our hangar, a full complement of pilots, and four operational Pilatus Porters, it seemed like the right time to get in there.

So last week, on an early Tuesday morning, my colleague Tim Harold and I flew a full load of Scriptures into Omban, the closest Ketengban airstrip to Onya. We unloaded the majority in Omban but left ten boxes of Old Testaments on the airplane for the people of Onya.

We then took off from Omban and headed northwest, following what the pilots here call the Long Valley. Looking down at the terrain below, I can only imagine how many days of hiking it would have taken Andrew to check this particular trek off his bucket list.

With the GPS showing us within a half mile of the airstrip, we still couldn't see it. Having never been there before, I wondered if perhaps we had the wrong coordinates, but I didn't have a good reason to believe our data was wrong. Besides, we'd followed what I remembered of Andrew's instructions to a tee: "From Omban, go out into the Long Valley and hang a left."

Just as my worry motor was firing up, Tim spotted part of the airstrip through the dissipating morning fog.

When the weather in these mountains calls for patience, patience is what you give it. With plenty of fuel on board, we circled overhead and got to know this little cul de sac off the Long Valley. As we circled, the fog steadily lifted, and soon the approach path was clearing nicely.

As we circled overhead, we finally spotted the Onya
airstrip as the early morning fog began to dissipate.
(Photo courtesy of Tim Harold)

Perched on a picturesque ridgeline, the community at Onya had done an excellent job subduing their mountain into an airstrip. After a couple of practice approaches, we were soon touching down on the smooth, firm surface.

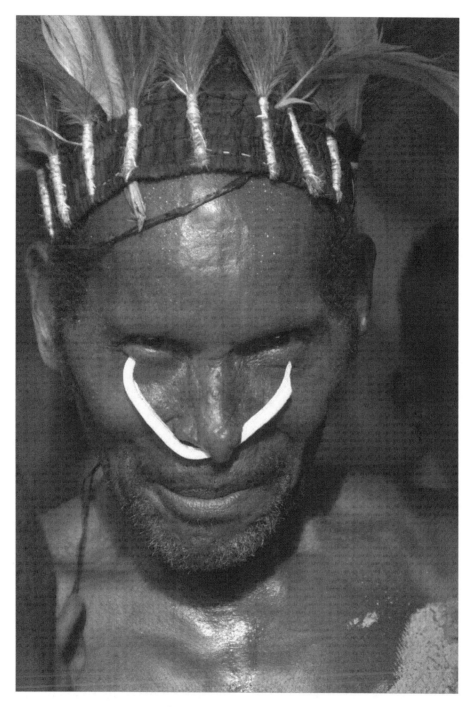

Dressed to celebrate. One of the men who
welcomed us after the first landing at Onya
(Photo courtesy of Tim Harold)

As soon as the prop stopped moving, the reception committee started a high-speed spin cycle around the aircraft with the now familiar Ketengban whooping overpowering our senses.

Once the mayhem settled down a bit, we had a short time of prayer, thanking God that these Scriptures had come to the people of Onya. After more than fifteen years out here, I'm finally catching on that ceremony is important, so we made one up on the spot.

On a remote outcropping in the Star Mountains of Papua, under the wing of an airplane that God's people gave specifically for this task, pastors and elders from the seven churches in the Onya valley received boxes filled with books that held the very words of their Creator.

Tim Harold delivers one of the boxes of
newly printed Ketengban Scriptures.

Looking at the crowd pressed in around the airplane, I guessed there were about a hundred Ketengban folk cheering each time a box came out of the airplane. My spiritual eyes don't work very well yet; otherwise, who knows, I might have been able to count the angels cheering as well.

Onya

60

CHEATERS

Whenever God's Word is spoken, read, or heard,
God himself is there.

—JOHN FRAME

A few weeks back, I flew into Pipal with an Indonesian missionary and boxes of the freshly printed Ketengban Scriptures, which are to be formally dedicated in June and distributed to the Ketengban believers at that time. In other words, these boxes are like Christmas presents that are supposed to sit under the tree, strictly off limits until Christmas morning.

But, it would seem that Pipal is populated with cheaters.

I have it on good authority that after the first day of sunup-to-sundown work constructing a home/ministry building at the top of the airstrip, the people brazenly broke the rules, removed a single Bible from one of the boxes, and implored our missionary friend to read from the Psalms and Proverbs. Exhausted from the hard day's work, he nonetheless complied (making him, at the very least, an accomplice in the cheating).

The people sat and listened as, for the first time in their valley's history, the ancient Hebrew words of David and Solomon were spoken in Ketengban. Many times, the missionary felt too tired to continue, but the people forced him to keep reading the contraband book late into the night.

The cheaters of Pipal continued to gather every night after work, hungry to repeat the wonder of hearing the Word of God in the language that had a clear and unobstructed shot at their hearts. And every night the cheaters forced our friend the missionary to read deep into the night, far past his endurance.

The aircraft that delivered the Bibles to Pipal just happened to be the plane that we had purchased in Nepal. From finding the aircraft to flying it in Papua was a long, challenging, expensive process. Likewise, the process of getting the Pipal airstrip operational was an enormous undertaking. The Indonesian missionary of this story has faced immense challenges along the way. The multiple man-years of blood, sweat, and tears poured into the translation project itself represent a stunningly high price to pay to produce a book. As I look at the level of expense in terms of time, energy, and money that it has taken to reach this tiny community in Pipal, I begin to shake my head and smile at the absolutely ridiculous economics of it all. How much for Psalms and Proverbs in the night?

And then, I am reminded of the immeasurable cost my God expended in searching out and finding me … a dirty rotten cheater like my friends in Pipal.

61

SEE

*To pray is to accept that we are, and always will be,
wholly dependent on God for everything.*
—Tim Keller

The last item on the pre-takeoff checklist was complete. I peered over the long snout of the Pilatus Porter only to see that the restless clouds had again closed off the narrow exit to the Omban valley. The trouble with Omban is that the steeply down-sloping airstrip points directly at a mountain wall. The valley takes a hard right turn at the end of the strip but, from the takeoff position at the top of the airstrip, all you see is the wall. Shutting down the engine, I decided to walk to the bottom of the airstrip and take a peek around the corner into the exit valley.

Standing at the edge of the cliff at the end of the runway, I could see around the corner—the valley was actually open quite nicely. I picked out a landmark on a ridge that I knew I'd be able to see from the top of the airstrip, turned around, and hiked back up to the airplane.

Arriving back at the top, I turned around and, to my chagrin, my go/no-go landmark was now enveloped in clouds. Ah well, when these mountains call for patience, patience is what you give them. My passengers were being extremely patient as well, agreeing to stay belted in their seats in anticipation of a brief window of open skies.

Forgive me, I should have introduced you to my passengers earlier. Andrew and Anne Sims have been working on Bible translation in

Papua's Star Mountains for more than twenty-five years. This particular week we were trying to pull off something that we'd never done before: Scripture dedications in three separate mountain locations—two different language groups—in a single week. Having had the first dedication in Omban two days prior, a huge gathering was waiting in nearby Okbap (along with two planeloads of guests) for the couple to arrive, so that the celebration could begin. Only thing was, we were trapped in Omban.

At the side of Omban's airstrip, a group of Ketengban were sitting, watching and waiting with us. Softly, one of the men in the group called over to me, "Hey, we're gonna pray if that's OK."

I'm sure they'd been waiting patiently for one of us professional Christians to think of it. Eventually their patience ran dry. *Somebody's got to do this.*

For several minutes this simple tribal man spoke fervently to the God he believed could understand his Ketengban sentences. The only words I understood were my name (probably in the context of, "Lord, forgive the idiot pilot who forgets to pray") and the Indonesian words for *airplane* and *weather*. And of course, the word *amen*, which, when uttered, was the signal for them all to open their eyes and look down the mountain slope to the valley's clogged mouth. Only, it wasn't clogged anymore. There was now a just-wide-enough opening, and my all-important landmark was clearly visible.

"See," the man says to me. Not a lot of emotion—just rock-sure faith that the Creator, as described in the Book we were dedicating, listens to his creation. Pointing at the opening in the clouds, he says, "God opened the weather for you."

I sputtered a thanks, climbed in, fired up and took off, not sure if this particular answer to prayer came with a "use before" date.

Recently, a friend asked what the highlight of those three dedications was for me. To be sure, there are many moments I will forever remember from that week of watching the Ketengban and Lik people celebrate God's Word in their own language, but the most powerful moment was a quiet one: having men of faith pray for us, and watching God answer that prayer.

62

BACON AND EGGS

Live simply.
Love generously.
—RONALD REAGAN

With a satisfying smack of the hammer, the last runway marker was pounded into the dirt and the job was done. Well, almost done. We still had to climb the hill.

For the Ngalum tribesmen helping mark their new airstrip at Diphikin, the walk back up to the top of their new airstrip is one of the easiest in their entire territory. A different story entirely for me, the middle-aged wimp whose middle-aged eyes are looking at the 14% grade that the middle-aged legs will have to walk up if his middle-aged self wants to get back to the airplane and fly home. Trudging up the hill, I do my best to mute the awful rasping that my middle-aged lungs are making, hoping to hide the racket from the maddeningly cheerful Ngalum beside me for whom this wouldn't even qualify as a Sunday stroll.

14%. The maximum grade for a road in mountainous areas of the United States is 7%. In Papua's Eastern Highlands you'll be hard-pressed to find a straight piece of land longer than 100 meters with only a 7% grade. For the Ngalum of Diphikin, the only reasonably straight piece of land suitable for an airstrip site just happens to have this ridiculous grade. Don't mind landing on it, not one bit. Walking up it is quite another matter.

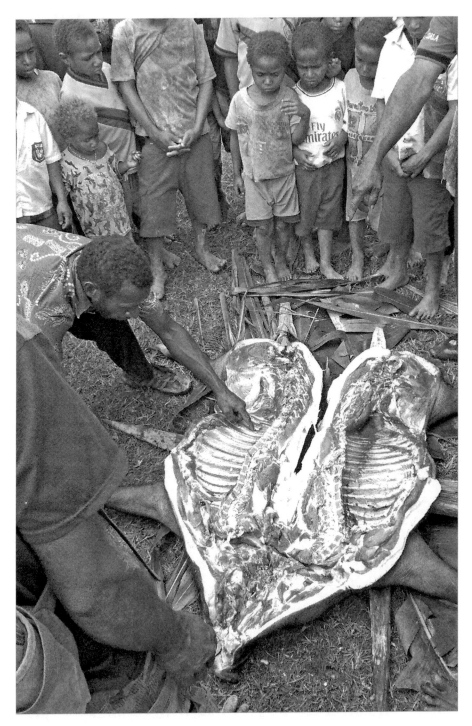

The pig was quickly dispatched and deftly butchered beside
the aircraft at the top of the airstrip at Diphikin.

To my delight, I don't pass out on the way up the hill. Cresting the top into the flat parking area, we arrive to find a hubbub in full kerfuffle. The folks who stayed at the top of the airstrip are butchering a large pig. A Ngalum man deftly uses an axe to do the job. They will send out the prized pork with me as gifts to our team in thanks for opening up their airstrip for service. A huge hind quarter has my name on it—they present it to me dripping with blood, ready for the grill. It's easily worth a month's salary in these parts, probably much more.

In the midst of this melee, a tiny little old woman weaves her way through the crowd carrying one of those ubiquitous little black plastic bags in her hands. She hands me her treasure gingerly. "For the pilot," she says, and disappears back into the crowd.

I peek in the bag. It's full of tiny eggs from her chickens. I can buy much larger eggs back in town for 15 cents apiece. But these are worth much more than money.

The woman at Diphikin gave these precious eggs to the undeserving, with no strings attached, and walked away with nothing but the sweetness of knowing her Master was smiling.

The pork is given with equal parts pure gratitude and hopeful expectation that we'll return the favor with frequent air service to the village. The eggs are given ... why? She knows I don't need them. She knows that I live like a king compared to her. I really don't know why she gave me those eggs. All I can think of is that she was simply being kind.

I continue to be blessed by these "little" people who belong to the Lord, scattered throughout the hinterlands of Papua. May I learn from them. May I grow to become like the little woman in Diphikin who gives to those who don't deserve, gives without strings attached, and walks away with nothing but the sweetness of knowing her Master is smiling.

63

OF WIND AND WAITING

The real problem with the world is not the bad things,
but the good things that have become the best thing.
—Tim Keller

A thousand feet above the ground, the wind skittered across the tops of the hills, giving us a mildly turbulent ride. The electronics in the instrument panel told me it was blowing at almost 20 knots. As we approached our destination from the east, it was clear that it would be unsafe to attempt a landing. A definite *no go*.

Our ministry is all about saying *yes. Yes* to transporting God's servants who have followed the call to serve in isolation and obscurity in Papua's jungles. *Yes* to the calls for medevacs. *Yes* to flying foul-smelling, ill-tempered pigs for a celebration of a new church. *Yes* to taking the time to help a village fix their broken radio.

But I often find that our *noes* are easily as significant as our *yeses*. When God's created order serves up unflyable weather or wind, the response of "no, not today" is simple common sense. But on another level, I think the decision to say "no, I can't" is quite something else: by it, we acknowledge our finiteness. Having weather change my plans demonstrates the limits of my vision. My Plan A for the day, as well-motivated as it may be, can differ radically from God's Plan A. I can attempt to force through my Plan A, or I can acknowledge my littleness, scrap Plan A and scurry for safe harbor. Plane and pilot are preserved to serve another day.

During Papua's windy season, there is often a period of calm for an hour or two just after sunrise. On this particular day, even though we had left Sentani as early as possible, the winds still beat us out of bed. Attempting to land on Tumdungbon's short, slippery, one-way airstrip with upwards of 15 knots of wind hustling us along from behind would have been beyond foolish. We made the easy decision and diverted to a nearby airstrip with a runway that allowed us to land into the wind. A Helivida* helicopter was going to be in the area that day, and the night before I had arranged with the pilot to be available to shuttle our passengers and cargo over to Tumdungbon if we were unable to get in ourselves.

Our passengers, two missionaries and a Nagi tribal woman whom they had been helping get medical treatment for tuberculosis, settled in for the wait. My colleague and I would wait until the helicopter was en route before leaving the missionaries and heading for home.

And now, God's Plan A for the day began to unfold.

First, a group of unhappy young men came purposefully striding up the airstrip to the airplane. The grudge they carried up the runway was soon set aside as a simple misunderstanding was rectified.

Next, Jerry emerged from the village with his trademark ear-to-ear grin that makes him such an engaging person. Jerry has been suffering with some kind of significant intestinal problem for a number of years, and the last time I had seen him I was flying his emaciated self out to town for medical treatment. He looked much better now, healed, happy, and with some much-needed meat on his bones. His eyes also glittered with the news that he was now married and had a healthy baby boy. He told me the story of how difficult the labor had been (a breach baby), and how God answered his fervent prayers for the safe arrival of his son. Before the child was born, Jerry had already chosen a name, but soon after the birth he had a dream in which he was reminded of the Lord's faithfulness during his extended time of suffering. Jerry scrapped his Plan A and followed the instruction he received in his dream, naming

Ayub: a baby in the wilds of Papua
named after the Biblical character Job

the boy Ayub (Job), as a testament to God's goodness in our times of suffering.

Jerry went and got his wife and came back to the airplane with their precious, living reminder of God's faithfulness. We talked for a while about how amazing Job was (the ancient one, not the dangerously diaper-less one on my arm). Neither green-pasture prosperity nor valley-of-death suffering were able to dislodge God from the center of his life. Encounters like this with genuine followers of Jesus in these remote areas are some of the most precious of God's gifts in this ministry.

After a while, Jerry excused himself to go back to teaching the village children. As he left, a family crossed the airstrip and headed off through the jungle in the direction of the river. The father carried his bow and arrows for hunting and his axe for woodcutting. The mom had her net bag hung over her back with the day's food, and in her hand was a home-made spear gun that would hopefully result in some fish or freshwater shrimp on the fire that evening. Their little girl came last, carrying a rattan fish trap. With not much else to do, I decided to tag along.

A short walk through the forest brought us to the confluence of a fair-sized stream with the main river. The family got into their canoe and took their leave downriver. Alone with my feet in the cool, crystal-clear water, I marveled at how God's Plan A for the day included the gifts of the conversation with Jerry and these unexpected moments of pure tranquility in a postcard-perfect setting.

Though my experience of the truths of Matthew 6:33 has been severely limited by my own stubborn disobedience, I continue to find Jesus to be good to his word: when we seek him first instead of other good things, the other good things come along too, and to me they seem to come at a time and in a manner that is much more satisfying than when I seek them directly.

64

THE GIRL AND THE BOX

Blessed are the poor in spirit.
—JESUS OF NAZARETH

After three and a half years in Papua, we were looking forward to heading home for a seven-month furlough. Things were wrapping up nicely. My next day at work was to be my last day of flying. A single out-and-back flight with a load of medical supplies for a team of doctors.

Then the phone rang.

Could I add one more flight? A woman from one of the interior villages had died, and her family was asking if we'd fly her body back home. Here was an opportunity for our team to show compassion to a grieving family. The answer was an easy yes.

The next morning, as the shadows gave way to the gentle light of a new day, our ground operations crew gingerly loaded the casket into the back of the Pilatus Porter. A man stood in the shadows watching. In his arms he held a little girl, perhaps 5 years old.

Caskets must not come in a standard size in Papua; this one was a bit wider than others I've flown. With the polished wooden box taking up most of the cabin, our guys were having trouble installing the seats. Leaving them to work on the problem, I walked over to the man in the shadows.

"Was she your wife?"

"Yes."

"I'm so sorry."

"And the little girl?" I nodded at the beautiful child clinging to his neck, still sleepy.

"She's my daughter."

We were quiet for a while, then walked over to the aircraft together. The team had planned for the two of them to sit together in the cabin alongside the casket, but they were only able to fit one seat into the seat tracks, all the way against the back wall of the cabin. I posed the dilemma to the father: Would his daughter rather ride up front next to me or in the back with the casket? He asked her the question in their native tongue. She shook her head vigorously. The father gave me a tired smile. She was more afraid of riding next to the scary foreigner than of sitting alone next to the box that held her mom's body.

She climbed up into that seat, alone in the back of the airplane. I fastened her seat belt and showed her how to open it. I began to pray for her. A little hand clutched mine and held on tight. When I finished, she smiled.

The girl and the box

I write these words a world away from the jungles of Papua. Comfortable, relaxed, and secure, I reflect on the ministry "back there." In the grand scheme of things, it often feels like we don't really accomplish that much. And that which we do accomplish? It takes an awful lot of effort. It takes an awful lot of money. It has more risk than I'd like. It wears people out.

Why go back?

The Lord brings this little girl to mind. I'll likely never see her again. I have no idea what her life will hold. But as I remember her, sitting next to her mother's coffin, squeezing my hand as we prayed, I sense the Lord saying that the ministry in Papua is measured by moments like this one. It's not measured by impressive lines on some graph. It is measured by unimpressive, unnoticed moments. Moments where the feeble faithfulness of a flawed team of men and women brings a taste of Jesus' unflawed love to one of his "least of these."

65

THE TENTH LEPER

Thou who has given so much to me,
give one thing more:
a grateful heart.
—GEORGE HERBERT

He spoke broken Indonesian, but I understood him well enough:

I have nothing with which to repay you.
God will reward you.

The words came from the lips of a grizzled old man as we stood under the wing of the plane at an isolated mountain airstrip. Tearful words of thanks for adding on a flight to fly his grieving family home after burying their son in a distant village.

It had been a long, hot, difficult day with multiple stops, long delays, lots of sweat, and not a few frustrations. At one point in the day's flying, I felt something moving on my stomach and looked down to see a cockroach running uphill on a beeline to get under my shirt sleeve. One of his relatives zipped across the instrument panel. They must have jumped ship from the evil-smelling sago I had hoisted aboard at the previous stop. I smushed the one on my shirt a few millimeters short of his destination. This didn't help the appearance of the shirt any, but I felt better. The day's difficulties, like the cockroaches, were multiple, ugly, and unwanted. They filled my senses, cried for the attention of my corruptible spirit, and clamored for me to conclude that life stinks.

And then the words of an old tribal man challenged me to see the unseen. To make real the unreal. To believe the unbelievable. That there is a God. That he is watching. That he delights when his children make feeble attempts at mimicking his love and mercy.

Papua is overrun with what I like to call "tenth lepers." Following in the footsteps of the original tenth leper who returned to Jesus to thank him for wiping the scourge from his skin, so many folks double back to say thanks to me for the smallest of things. The most creative thanks I have ever received was written on a roll of toilet paper and left prominently on my desk: appreciation from missionaries whose massive shipment of the vital stuff I'd frantically stashed in a dry water tank by the side of the runway during a tropical downpour.

What about me? What about you? Are we one of the nine? Or do we, like number 10, take the time to look around us and marvel at the healing that God has done on our leprous hearts? Do we shake our heads in wonder at the goodness God allows into our lives despite the fact that we live in a horribly broken place?

I'm jarred by a man who, having just buried his son, still doubled back to thank the pilot who has known no such suffering. I flew home counting the ways that God has already rewarded me. I was struck by the privilege our team has of being involved in so many different ministries, the privilege of touching so many lives, the privilege of getting a God's eye view of one of the most beautiful, pristine places left on the planet, the privilege of knowing that as a result of our collective efforts, the Word of God will remain in this place long after we are gone. I found myself doubling back to my Master to ask for forgiveness for thinking that life isn't fair because a cockroach is making a run for my armpit.

Then I thanked him for his unfairness towards me: he showers good things on the undeserving.

66

ORCHIDS IN THE DITCH

There's not a plant or flower below
but makes thy glories known.
—ISAAC WATTS

As I've stated before, in the jungles of Papua, the men's room is always easy to find: it's located any place not currently being used as a lady's room. And so it was at Sekame—no fancy signage, just a couple of bushes next to the ditch at the side of the airstrip, and I had found the vital facilities I was looking for.

On the floor of the ditch, something caught my eye as being out of place. Here, standing tall among the dirt and the weeds, were wild orchids in all their delicate, regal beauty.

Orchids in the ditch. Considered by some the most beautiful flowers in the world. Costly, sought after, highly prized. And here they are, in a ditch.

The thing is, the orchids didn't know they were in a ditch. There they were, doing exactly what they were put on earth to do: bloom. They were shouting out God's creative brilliance, his love of beauty, and his desire for us to be enraptured by that beauty. And they are doing all this *in a ditch*, just like they would if they were the centerpiece attraction at a world-class botanic garden being oohed and aahed over by professional flower people.

I took some of the orchids from the ditch home to Sheri—
they ended up flourishing on our front porch in Sentani.

I pay way too much attention to the context in which I find myself. Am I willing to fulfill what God has me on earth to do when I find myself in some anonymous ditch in a backwater village deep in the interior of Papua? Or do I put in the effort to shine only when I have an audience of professional Christian people from whom I might coax an ooh or aah?

Am I willing to shout out God's creative brilliance, the beauty of who he is, by producing my best work and allowing joy to rule in my heart even when all I see around me is dirt, weeds, and the steep walls of the ditch I'm in?

Thank you, God, for orchids in the ditches.

67

AN UNWRINKLED NOSE

Service which is rendered without joy
helps neither the servant nor the served.
—MAHATMA GANDHI

I walked from the airplane to the bundle on the ground. The first thing I noticed was the flies. Then the smell. The smell was the smell of death, and it drew the flies that flew vulture circles around the perfectly still figure of a tiny woman, still alive, the image of God clinging tenaciously to her exhausted features. All that is evil and broken in this world sought to mercilessly destroy this weak and weary image-bearer.

She'd been carried on a makeshift litter over the steep mountain trail from a nearby village to reach the airstrip where my airplane was now parked. Her husband stood beside her, holding another bundle in his hands, a *noken*—one of the net bags woven from tree bark fibers that his people have been making for as long as anyone has memory of this place. I peered into the noken. It contained perhaps the most uncorrupted vision of the image of God we're likely to see on this broken planet: the woman's perfect newborn child.

While the child's mother lay on the ground struggling for life, her baby slept serenely in his father's arms. The miracle of childbirth, cursed when our race turned away from God, now threatened the life of the baby's young mother.

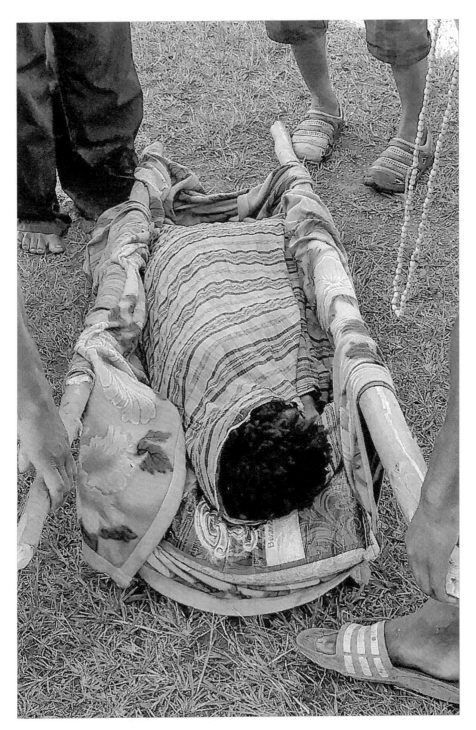

Carried over the mountain trail on a makeshift stretcher,
the young mother hovered near death's door.

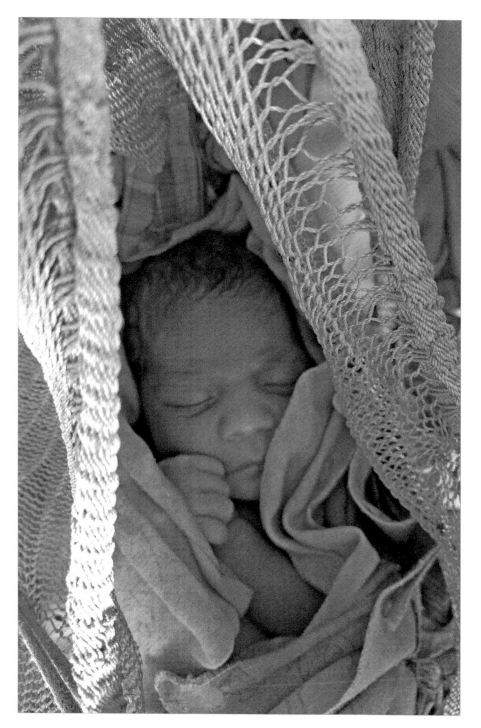

The woman's healthy newborn,
a perfect specimen of the image of God

Stepping out of the airplane in Sentani, I went to help one of our ground staff with the stretcher. As we gently moved our patient from the airplane to the stretcher, I watched my coworker's face as the stench hit him.

Not a flinch.

Not the tiniest wrinkling of the nose. I knew that the only reason he didn't react to his senses was out of respect for this little tribal woman, wrapped in filthy, blood-soaked blankets. You don't wrinkle your nose at someone you believe carries God's image.

Our team had to navigate some really rough waters this particular year. At that moment under the wing of the PC-6, watching my colleague restrain the very natural instinct to gag, my heart leapt and said,

Yes! This is it. This is why we're here.

*This is why we fight on. This is why we don't quit
when everything in us wants to.*

*As a flawed and broken team, we're somehow being used
to touch the least of God's image-bearers.*

68

THEY WILL INHERIT THE EARTH

*The regalia of the kings that God has anointed
are their troubles, their sorrows, and their griefs.*
—CHARLES SPURGEON

Getting checked out as a missionary pilot in Papua involves a lot more than learning how to land on short, slippery runways or navigate mountain passes. For many of us, learning to interact well with the many different people groups of Papua is a steep learning curve. In the preceding weeks, I had passed along as much knowledge I could dig out of my aging mind to my new colleague, Andy.

We had just landed at a mountain runway, and it was now time for me to quit getting in the way and allow him to handle a complete "turn-around"—the time we spend on the ground at a remote village—on his own.

With Andy doing all the work, I was freed up to enjoy some extended time with my friend Pies who had showed up at the airplane that morning. I turned to Pies and said, "Let's take a walk through the village." He led me down the path into the picturesque village of Maksum. Pies' wife had died in this village a number of years prior (see chapter 21, "The Wrong Airplane"). Weaving our way through the patchwork of huts, Pies and I caught up on each other's lives. Floating through the open doorways came smoke from the morning cooking fires and the warm Ketengban greeting, *Telebe.* I felt among family.

Pies met me after we landed in Maksum.

As we approached the center of the village, I noticed a large, obviously temporary thatch-roofed structure that had been erected in the center of the village. I asked Pies about it. "That's where I'm taking you," he replied.

Pies began to explain that one of their elders had just passed away. The large hut is where folks could gather and pass the hours of mourning together. Most of the mourners had gone up to meet the arrival of our flight, but a few men were still gathered around a fire chatting quietly.

"He must have been an important person." Half statement, half question, I waited for Pies to respond.

"Yes, he was." Pies' eyes lit up. "Gerson was the first person to receive the good news in Maksum. When the missionaries first came, Gerson protected them from hostility and told our people that we needed to listen to the message these strange people were bringing into the valley."

Pies continued, saying that Gerson was the first person in Maksum transformed by the gospel of Jesus Christ. He turned away from the darkness that had gripped his people for millennia and towards the light of a restored relationship with his Creator. Gerson spent the rest of his

Pies led me to the hut where Gerson's body was lying in state.

life encouraging his people to do the same. And they had responded. It was obvious to me how cherished this man was to his people.

Instead of heading to the mourning area, Pies grabbed my arm and led me down a side path to a different hut. Inside, in a handmade coffin of rough wooden planks, lay Gerson's empty shell. On a rough shelf in the corner there's a book—a reminder that Gerson lived to see the day when God's Word could be read in his Ketengban language. Some of his family sat on the floor around the coffin. They would bury him later that day.

I expressed my condolences, asked a few questions, and took a photograph. As I put my phone back in my pocket, I was reminded of images of the kings lying in state. Gilded caskets, honor guards, vaulted cathedrals, the world's leaders lining up to pay their respects ... and here? In a simple hut, in a tiny, isolated village, totally hidden from the view of the powerful of this world, I can't help but wonder if I'm looking at one who will be a king in the next version of this world.

Blessed are the meek,
for they will inherit the earth.

69

Gone Are the Illusions

*Spread your sail toward the storm
and trust in him who rules the raging seas.*
—John Ross MacDuff

I had just finished my first week back on the job in Papua after a time in the United States. One thing that strikes me with renewed freshness is the sheer impossibility of what we're trying to do out here. Two hundred seventy different people groups scattered across 153,000 square miles of deep jungle, swamp, and mountains. The physical barriers are almost as difficult to traverse as the staggering linguistic and cultural divides. And we're trying to be a part of reaching them with a small group of diverse missionaries and five little airplanes? Ludicrous.

But the enormity of the job isn't what really gives me pause. It's how fragile and tenuous a hold that this partnership of weak and sometimes faithless disciples have on this beachhead, particularly when I look up at the mountains facing us and consider the list of things that would threaten to undo us. It's not the passive opposition of the impassable terrain, the enormity of the task, or the limited resources that are the most daunting—it's the active opposition, in its seemingly endless variety of forms, that strives to keep us from moving off the beach at all. From my limited human perspective, there simply is no way we will succeed in what we have set out to do here.

Earlier this week, as I was praying about the challenges facing us, I was struck by the stark contrast between the relatively manageable and straightforward life I'd just left in the States, and the ridiculously huge challenges facing a small group of weak and flawed followers of Jesus out here at the end of the earth. The interesting thing was that while most of my cowardly person wanted to run and hide (and maybe make things spiritual by praying for a David to come slay our Goliath), some small portion of my soul didn't shrink back from this totally untenable situation. As crazy as it sounds, the part of me that actually smiled at the mountain of challenges was saying something like, "It is really good to be back where there are no illusions of success without the powerful intervention of God."

Obviously, you don't have to leave your home country to put yourself in a position of ridiculous dependence on God, but you do have to surrender to following Jesus wherever he leads. And I can promise you he'll lead you away from the safety and security of your comfort zone to a better place. A place of sweet and utter dependence on him.

70

MARBATA MAMA

I live in a high and holy place,
but also with the one who is contrite and lowly in spirit.
—ISAIAH 57:15

After 30 minutes of hiking pretty much nonstop uphill, we came to a bit of a clearing. I looked back at the airstrip where we had started, now clearly in view. We had made it to the ridgeline that marks the last section of the final approach to Omban's short runway. My mind did some quick math: the airplane passes over this point 10 seconds before touchdown. It had taken us 30 minutes to cover the same ground.

We were hiking from Omban to Marbata to take a look at the airstrip the community had just finished building. The two villages were 2 minutes apart as the airplane flies. So, if it had taken us 30 minutes to cover 10 seconds of flight-time, at this rate we should get there in… The math made my head hurt.

Five hours later, when we crested the last of many hills and finally saw the hamlet of Marbata, my head still hurt, but not as much as the rest of me.

There are hundreds of isolated communities in Papua's rugged mountainous interior whose people make hikes far longer than ours to get to the nearest airstrip for access to supplies, medicine, education, and a connection to the outside world.

Thirty minutes into the hike with Pastor Andi.
The airstrip at Omban is in the background.

The people of Marbata were willing to literally move part of their mountain to eliminate that isolation. My colleague Mark and I had made the hike from the closest existing airstrip to ensure that they had sufficiently rearranged the mountain to make landing an expensive 5,000-pound projectile on it a relatively safe proposition.

The welcoming committee was something that is better experienced than described. Ecstatic. Rhythmic. Deafening.

Once the hubbub had somewhat subsided, they led us to a roofed platform that they had built especially for the occasion. The pastor who had made the hike with us from Omban (and didn't appear to have broken a sweat in the process) pulled out his Bible to share from the Word of God. The entire community sat on the airstrip to listen. While we were waiting for the pastor to get started, a tiny old woman slowly climbed the steps to the platform and came over to Mark and me. She had an ancient face, but her eyes sparkled. Someone translated the words she spoke:

The welcoming committee at Marbata

I have been praying that before I die,
God would allow our airstrip to be opened.
Thank you for coming. I will die in peace.

***

Four weeks after walking through the mountains to inspect the runway at Marbata, I had the privilege of returning. This time I took the easy way, landing an airplane on Marbata's runway for the first time. I marveled again at the amount of work these industrious people had accomplished. They had moved truckload upon truckload of earth, by hand. Crowbars—and sticks sharpened to impersonate crowbars—were their only tools.

After working with the community to install runway markers, we were preparing to leave when I saw a familiar figure shuffling across the top of the runway towards the airplane, steadied on the arm of her adult daughter. She looked feebler than when I'd last seen her a month ago, and her eyes seemed to have lost some of their sparkle.

"Her eyes had lost some of their sparkle, and she was a bit
unsteady on her feet. Her incredible faith still moves me."

Looking toward heaven, she said, "I prayed, and God heard."

Reaching the airplane, she clasped my hand. She came to thank us again, but this was my time to speak.

Mama, you prayed that God would allow your runway
to be opened before you go to heaven.
God heard your prayers.
He listens to you, just like he listens to me.

The folks standing around us did a quick translation. I saw the flash of recognition on her face, and those eyes sparkled once again. Speaking with passion, she pointed her walking stick at the heavens and said:

I prayed, and God heard.

71

THE DELEGATION

It is something to be a follower, however feeble,
in the wake of the Great Teacher.
—Dr. David Livingstone

I couldn't sleep. The long hike into Marbata, the celebration, the runway inspection, the pig feast, and the icy bath in the stream were all behind us. It was night now. I was bone-tired and desperately ready for sleep.

I had a decent sleeping mat and the woven floor of the hut had enough spring in it to be comfortable, but the rhythmic beat of the dancers' feet outside the door and the cadence of their chants kept my brain from shutting down for the night. That, and the embers in the fire pit in the center of the hut were making it uncomfortably warm. I glanced over at Mark, the only other occupant of our sleeping quarters. He appeared to be dozing soundly under a mosquito net. Thinking uncharitable thoughts about him, the dancers, and the embers, I stripped down to my boxers and once again shut my eyes.

Time passed, and sleep still eluded me. I heard some rustling and figured Enos had come in. I knew he and another companion from the hike were going to share the hut with us that night.

Sometime later, still unable to sleep, I rolled over, and in the process, I must have accidentally jostled open my heavy eyelids. In the glow of the fire pit, I could make out a stunning image: a group of men, seated in a semicircle around me.

The one closest to me spoke my name. It was Demi. By now the once-droopy eyelids stood at full attention having auto-adjusted to the position commonly referred to as wide open. I counted twelve men in the hut. I'm not sure how long Demi would have waited for me to open my eyes, but my guess is a very, very long time—the Ketengban do not share their Western brothers' lack of patience. Whipping on a t-shirt, I made a mental note to find my bucket list and cross off "opening eyes to find self surrounded by twelve men while self clad only in boxers."

Demi, a longtime friend who helped with the New Testament translation for his Ketengban people, explained that these men were the elders from three distant villages. They had hiked through the mountains—some of them had been on the trail for days—to get to Marbata, because they had heard through the jungle grapevine that Mark and I would be here. One by one the elders made their case, pleading with me to come to their villages and open the runways their people had built.

I listened to these dear men speak with earnestness and humility. When it was time for me to speak, I wished that I could promise them something. All I could do was attempt to convey how much our team cared for each of their communities, but what a huge undertaking opening each new runway was for us, and how limited our capacity was as a team.

We talked deep into the night. Eventually we spent some time praying together, asking the God we all worshiped to make a way for their runways to be opened and their communities to begin to benefit from the ministry of the aircraft. Each man then filed past my sleeping mat, and we shook hands before they slipped out the door into the night.

I looked over at Mark's corner of the hut. He was still dozing peacefully. More uncharitable thoughts...

***

I write this sitting at a kitchen table a world away from that hut deep in the Star Mountains of Papua. Sheri and I miss many things about living and ministering in Papua, but near the top of the list has got to be the opportunity to fellowship with dear believers like those men in the night. Believers who, though so radically different from us, love the same Lord, and inspire us with their patience, endurance, and joy in the midst of lives much more difficult than our own.

Afterword

Twenty-two years after we crossed the Pacific in the upper deck of that Boeing 747, we found ourselves recrossing that ocean, eastbound this time, and in economy. We'd made numerous trips back to the States during our time in Papua, but this one was different. We embarked on all of our previous journeys with our return date to Papua already set, often with roundtrip tickets in hand. This time our tickets were one-way, and we'd left Papua uncertain when we might return.

Without knowing whether the Papua chapter of our lives is over or not, it still seems an appropriate time to reflect on the journey that God graciously allowed us to take thus far. Many have encouraged us to share some of what we saw God do in Papua more broadly—to write a book—and so, the time seemed right to do just that.

The stories recorded here, for the most part, don't reflect the mundane routines of daily living, the times of discouragement, conflict, and failure. There's no chapter dedicated to the hours of tedious paperwork, drafting manuals, working on budgets, or writing emails. There's the risk that the reader may come away from this volume with the false impression that life as a missionary pilot with YAJASI is an uninterrupted string of exciting days, each containing an interesting story or spiritual lesson. Umm … no. A ton of daily life happened between the chapters of this book. And, quite honestly, there were many difficult days—days when the only reason we stayed was a simple exercise of the will (and perhaps because Sheri and I never could quite get our act together and both decide to quit on the same day). And so, while recognizing that these stories don't tell the whole story, they very much tell *the heart of the story*. These stories gave us undeserved and unpromised glimpses of God at work.

I now work on the home front, at JAARS, where our journey to serve with YAJASI in Papua started over twenty-five years ago. From the JAARS Center in Waxhaw, North Carolina, we support the frontline work of teams such as YAJASI all over the world. The heart of the JAARS mission statement is:

making Bible translation possible
in the most remote and difficult places on earth

Many of the *places* where the gospel has yet to gain a foothold, and where the Word of God remains out of reach, are *remote and difficult*. These places are often bypassed, ignored, or forgotten by a world that increasingly passes them by. But God has not forgotten the people who call these remote and difficult places home. Indeed, he has made it clear in his Word that he has plans to redeem image-bearers from all people groups, no matter how remote or difficult their location.

It's also clear that God's plan to redeem people from every corner of his earth involves having some of his disciples cross the difficult physical, geographic, linguistic, and cultural boundaries and go to these remote and difficult places. By definition, this can't be all of us … but some of us must go. In Papua alone, there remain somewhere in the neighborhood of one hundred people groups who do not have the Word of God in their language, every one of them located in a remote and difficult place. Should you go? God is certainly calling some of you to go. The rest of you he's calling to get involved. I'm a pilot, not a missiologist or theologian, but being blissfully ignorant of any rules prohibiting airplane drivers from reading the Bible, the pattern I see in its pages is that the entire body of Christ is to participate in missionary enterprise.

Some went. The others sent. All had skin in the game.

For those God may be calling to go, it's quite possible you will find very few reasons to convince yourself to actually go. You'll likely be able to quickly produce an extensive list of excellent reasons why you shouldn't. If the top of your "shouldn't go" list centers on your own limitations, you're in excellent biblical company. But, as with Moses or Mary, God isn't really interested in your view of yourself. God is interested in your view of *him*. To reach the people of the earth's remote and difficult regions, it's my belief that God wants to use ordinary folks who have an extraordinary view of their God.

It's also my experience, and the experience of countless others, that while the missionary endeavor is difficult—every real adventure has real danger, real disappointment, real loss—those who respond to God's call to be part of reaching these people are rewarded with a unique front-row seat to watching God at work.

It's Sheri's and my hope, our prayer, that God might in a small way use these stories to draw some of his people to go.

Go to the remote and difficult places.

Acknowledgements

Attempting to recognize all who have made this book possible should come with hazard pay—I'm certain to inadvertently omit some to whom I'm indebted. But since the stories in the preceding chapters owe their existence to a host of people not named me, it's a risk that must be taken.

Getting an aircraft airborne at the end of the earth is a massive undertaking. Every time the airplane I was flying touched down in a remote Papuan village, a huge team of people had already performed their jobs flawlessly in order to make that landing possible.

YAJASI's team of aviation maintenance technicians maintain aircraft to the highest of standards despite operating in a remote and challenging context. YAJASI's flight coordinators, flight followers, and ground operations staff oversee a complex aviation operation that ensures YAJASI's resources are efficiently directed towards meeting the needs of the people of Papua. The administrative team at YAJASI perform the equally complex (and often thankless) task of ensuring that the bills are paid, the facility maintained, and the myriad permits, permissions, licenses, visas, and airworthiness certificates are issued.

In 1995 the YAJASI Board stuck their necks out and invited Sheri and me to join the ministry in Papua. Thank you for giving us the opportunity to serve with you and the rest of the YAJASI team. May God bless your diligent work as you shepherd the ongoing ministry.

Standing behind YAJASI is JAARS—an absolutely vital partner in making the aviation team's efforts at the end of the earth successful. In particular, the aviation training team at JAARS has had a significant impact on the work of YAJASI. Thank you for equipping us so well for the difficult job of flying in Papua.

Woody McLendon, president of JAARS, saw the value of a book that told what God is doing through aviation in Papua and took the considerable risk of greenlighting this project.

A team of individuals and churches have partnered for years with Sheri and me, standing behind our ministry, sacrificially ensuring that we could follow God's call on our lives to Papua. Thank you. Many of you have encouraged us to write this book—these are your stories.

If you found this book at all readable, that would be Carol Brinneman's doing. Carol shepherded this work from the outset, and her fingerprints are on every page. Her finely tuned editing instincts served me incredibly well—she patiently spent many an hour cleaning up the messes my keyboard never failed to produce. Carol's depth of experience in seeing a writing project through from start to finish was invaluable.

I'm very grateful for the expert layout skills that Joyce Hyde brought to the job. As a first-time author, it was such a privilege for me to have someone as experienced as Joyce work her magic on this manuscript and turn it into a real-life, hold-it-in-your-hand book.

I would never have started writing were it not for the encouragement of my best friend, my wife, Sheri. Sheri heard these stories first at our dinner table as I shared the highlights of the day's flying. Her faith-fueled excitement at hearing what God was doing inspired me to take the time to commit the dinner-table ramblings to writing. Sheri never wavered in her belief that the stories needed to see the light of day. She served as my initial editor, sounding board, critic, and encourager-in-chief. Her faith, perseverance, and raw grit saw us through many a difficult day. Her cheerfulness and laughter made the sunny days along the way even brighter. This book exists because I have graciously been given a wife with a passion for God, a love for the downtrodden, and a calling to the end of the earth.

GLOSSARY

call-out

Air crews call out key events, such as passing a committal point, during the course of a flight. Most call-outs occur during the takeoff and landing phases of flight.

cargo pod

An additional cargo compartment, usually constructed out of fiberglass, designed to increase an aircraft's cargo capacity. Most cargo pods are attached to the belly of the aircraft. The Helio Courier's belly cargo pod, which was designed by JAARS, can be seen in the photo in chapter 11. JAARS also designed underwing cargo pods for the Pilatus Porter, greatly increasing the utility of that aircraft—one of these underwing pods is visible in the background of the photo on page 200.

flare for landing

Just prior to touchdown, a pilot pitches the nose of the aircraft upwards, increasing the amount of lift generated by the aircraft's wings and slowing the aircraft's rate of descent to achieve a smooth landing.

Helimission/Helivida

A Switzerland-based helicopter ministry. We had the privilege of working closely with Helimission since they began flying in Papua in the late 1990s. Their vital work is now carried out by Helivida Indonesia.

Helio Courier

Designed to deliver excellent takeoff and landing performance on short, rough runways, these unique single-engine aircraft were the workhorses of our fleet for almost thirty years. Chapter 11, "Reunions," contains a fuller description of the Helio Courier (page 57).

hot refueling

Refueling a helicopter without shutting down the engine.

inclinometer

A handheld tool for measuring slope or grade. Also called a clinometer.

preflight inspection

An inspection performed by pilots prior to their first flight in an aircraft to assure that the aircraft is airworthy.

tailwind

Wind coming from the direction behind the aircraft. On takeoff, tailwinds can dramatically increase the distance required for an aircraft to get airborne, and on landing, tailwinds similarly increase the distance required to stop the aircraft.